EARCH OF THE
ANISH TRAIL

TO LOS ANGELES, 1829-1848

DOLORES PUBLIC LIBRARY
P.O. BOX 847
DOLORES, CO 81323

Dolores page 33-38 (40)

Spanish Trail ford of the Green River as sketched by R. H. Kern, artist with the Gunnison Survey, 1853.

IN SEARCH OF THE SPANISH TRAIL

Santa Fe to Los Angeles, 1829-1848

C. Gregory Crampton and Steven K. Madsen

GIBBS·SMITH

P

PUBLISHER

Salt Lake City

97 96 95 94 6 5 4 3 2 1

Text, photographs and maps ©1994 by C. Gregory Crampton and Steven K. Madsen

This is a Peregrine Smith book,
published by Gibbs Smith, Publisher,
P.O. Box 667
Layton, Utah 84041

Photograph Sources
Photographs for this book have been supplied by C. Gregory Crampton, unless otherwise credited following the caption.

Design by Warren Archer, Salt Lake City, Utah
Maps drawn by Don Bufkin, Tucson, Arizona

Manufactured in the United States of America

Library of Congress Cataloging in Publication Data

Crampton, C. (Charles Gregory), 1911-
    In Search of the Spanish Trail: Santa Fe to Los Angeles,
1829-1848 / C. Gregory Crampton and Steven K. Madsen
            p.   cm.
    Includes bibliographical references and index.
    ISBN 0-87905-614-2 (pbk.) : $24.95
    1. Old Spanish Trail. 2. Southwest, New—History—To 1848.

I. Madsen, Steven K., 1949-, joint author. II. Title.
F787.C73 1994   94-18621
979—dc20   CIP

PREFACE

In this book, we have mapped the Spanish Trail in detail for the first time. The Spanish Trail was a 1,120-mile-long, northward-looping trace between Santa Fe and Los Angeles, a commercial route used by traders operating during the Mexican period, 1829-1848. It passed through six states—New Mexico, Colorado, Utah, Arizona, Nevada, and California—one of the most scenic regions of the United States. Contemporary with the Oregon and Santa Fe trails, it was the first major thoroughfare across the Southwest.

Until now, very little has been known about the trail itself. The first major study of the Spanish Trail was published in 1954 by LeRoy and Ann Hafen. This background work emphasized the political, economical, and international factors, but the trail was identified only in general terms. The public perception of the old pack route has remained blurred and illusory.

There is an archaeological urgency in making this study. The intrusion of modern man has obliterated much of the historic route. New roads are covering old trails. Energy-related mining, wide-scale farming, reclamation and power projects, gas-line construction, and ever-increasing use of off-road and recreational vehicles are rapidly eroding the fragile trail in those sections where it may still be seen.

To produce the maps in this book, we traveled the entire trail from Santa Fe to Los Angeles. Our primary purpose was to map the main trail as it was known during the peak time of its use, about 1840. We used passenger cars, pickups, and four-wheel drives. On several occasions, we used light aircraft to get an overview of portions of the trail not easily visible from the ground, and of course we walked, and walked, and walked.

Data collected during the field studies were recorded on topographic maps, published by the U.S. Geological Survey. These maps, meeting national map accuracy standards, blanket the trail's entire course.

The question is asked, "How do you follow a horse trail that is well over a hundred years old?" Although the trail saw heavy through-traffic during its 20-year life, those who ran the trading caravans provide little information about its location. Record-keeping contemporary trail riders are few in number. John C. Frémont covered a lengthy section of the trail in 1844, and his work is a significant primary source. George Brewerton and Kit Carson followed the route in 1848; Brewerton's account of the trip was published in 1853. Only one contemporary traveler, Orville Pratt, who followed the entire route from New Mexico to California, kept a complete diary. Although there were several hundred people involved in trail drives through the years, we must assume that they were either too busy to write or were illiterate. To verify the route, therefore, we must rely on additional sources. Much of what we know about the route and the trailside environment comes to us from the writings of travelers in post-trail days, who were aware they were traversing the Spanish Trail, and accurately identified and described it.

The writings of official government explorers, following limited or extended segments of the old trail, help us document the route with considerable accuracy. Frémont tells us that he is following the Spanish Trail. Therefore, if we can follow Frémont, we can locate the trail. In another instance, John W. Gunnison tells us in 1853 that he is following a portion of the Spanish Trail. He describes his travel in precise terms; therefore, using his data, we can locate the Spanish Trail. The Macomb expedition of 1859 gives us the Spanish Trail's location for nearly 300 miles. Maps made by the Wheeler and Hayden surveys also plot the Spanish Trail for hundreds of miles. And there were others.

Our job was to apply this accumulated data to our explorations in the field. Thus, on the ground we followed, or attempted to follow, these and later explorers. Occasionally, one of these trusted guides led us astray, but our on-the-ground investigation corrected their unintentional mistakes.

Where we had no prior guidance, we steered a course between two known points, determined by geographical considerations. Our findings are plotted on the twelve maps here published. The sources we used—manuscripts, published works, and maps—are cited in the bibliography. The vital contributions made by individuals and institutions will be noted below.

We did not set out to write a guidebook, but we have highlighted many places of interest in a region distinguished by its rich cultural and geographical diversity. We have kept the armchair traveler and the modern explorer in mind as we follow an east-west orientation in our study. Traversing the Spanish Trail, the modern traveler may visit national parks and monuments, and state parks, museums, and libraries. Trail seekers today may also view prehistoric ruins and paleontological sites, and may drive through Indian villages, mining and railroad towns, Mormon villages, and Spanish settlements. What is most important is that today's traveler, in addition to trailside attractions, may view firsthand the vanishing remains of the trail itself.

In these pages, we have introduced the major literature descriptive of the Spanish Trail. We refer to some of the main sources in the text and notes. Given the length of the trail, the literature we found pertinent to its several sections adds up to a lengthy bibliography. Anyone planning to write more extensively about the trail, or any of its parts, will find these sources of primary interest. For the convenience of modern trail followers, we have divided the route of the Spanish Trail into twelve sections or chapters, roughly equal in length, each with a corresponding map and photographic illustrations.

Those who wish to see the trail firsthand may retrace short stretches with some accuracy in passenger cars. Other lengths, back from the pavement, may require the use of four-wheel-drive vehicles. Some remote sections can only be followed on horseback or on foot. Modern explorers should consult accurate maps, preferably the topographical quadrangle maps issued by the U.S. Geological Survey.

A word about lost mines and buried treasure. It would be an exercise in futility for anyone to look for Spanish gold along the Spanish Trail. There is no reliable evidence suggesting that travelers on the contemporary Spanish Trail were carrying, or burying, or prospecting for, either gold or silver. In the event that you find a buried treasure, please notify the authors (so that we may include the information in a subsequent edition!)

This work resulted from extensive library and archival research and exploration in the field which began in June 1976. The people and institutions listed here contributed information, assistance, guidance, companionship, and in various ways greatly contributed to the fun we had in writing this book.

For their assistance, we gratefully acknowledge: W. L. "Bud" Rusho, Don Cecala, Henry J. Webb, Phil Martin, Gibbs M. Smith, Herman U. Butt, C. S. Cecil Thomson, S. Alva Matheson, Elbert L. Cox, Robert W. Delaney, Henry A. Huish, Sherwin "Scoop" Garside, Harold A. Steiner, F. A. and Mary M. Barnes, Joe W. and Jacqueline S. Gelo, James R. Hinds, Robert R. "Bob" Norman, Dennis L.

Jenkins, Carolyn Grattan, John L. Jackson, Gregory C. Thompson, James L. Kimball, Jr., Wilford Murdock, and Raymond Wheeler.

We appreciate the assistance of librarians, ranchers, educators, business people, and government employees who supplied information and were helpful in other ways: John L. Jorgensen, Charles S. Peterson, Pearl Baker, William B. Smart, Patricia McCarthy, Blanche Clegg, Herbert Davis, Harold Schindler, A. Reed Sommerville, Milton Harvey Williams, Chris Gomez, Joe Ben Wheat, Gerald A. Smith, Lloyd and Marian Pierson, Kenneth C. and Lucinda Ruth W. Madsen, D. W. Lowe, Lynn and Evelyn Ishmael, G. Clell Jacobs, James H. Knipmeyer, Jay M. Haymond, Mike Hartless, Craig E. Johansen, Art Martinez, Otho Murphy, Elizabeth Nichols, Harold L. Boyer, Marion S. Albrechtsen, S. Lyman Tyler, Jack C. Peterson, John W. Rockwell, John Mahon, Todd I. Berens, Max P. Erickson, and Bonnie Bell.

We give special thanks to our wives, Mary Helen P. Crampton and N. Adrienne Packard Madsen, for their patience and support of research and writing. They were good companions on several long segments of the old trail.

We are indebted to the dedicated staff of the following institutions: Department of History, and Department of Anthropology, Museum of New Mexico, Santa Fe; Bureau of Land Management offices in Santa Fe, Sacramento, Las Vegas, Phoenix, Cedar City and Salt Lake City, Utah, Barstow, California; county recorder's offices in Castle Dale, Monticello, Moab, in Utah, Cortez and Durango in Colorado; Utah State Land Office, Salt Lake City; Center of Southwest Studies, Fort Lewis College, Durango, Colorado; Western History Department, Denver Public Library, Denver, Colorado; Dan O'Laurie Museum, Moab, Utah; Fish Lake National Forest supervisor's office, Richfield, Utah; Special Collections, Dickinson Library, University of Nevada, Las Vegas; Dixie College Library, St. George, Utah; Nevada State Historical Society and Nevada Museum, Las Vegas; Nevada State Historical Society, Reno; San Bernardino County Museum, San Bernardino, California; Huntington Library, San Marino, California; National Archives and Records Service, Washington, D.C.; Library of Congress, Washington, D.C.; Bancroft Library, University of California, Berkeley; U.S. Geological Survey offices, Salt Lake City and Washington, D.C.; Utah State Historical Society, Salt Lake City; Archives Division, Historical Department, Church of Jesus Christ of Latter-day Saints, Salt Lake City, Utah; Special Collections, Marriott Library, Utah Engineering and Experiment Station, University of Utah, Salt Lake City; Jicarilla Apache Tribal Government offices, Dulce, New Mexico; Fort Irwin Military Reservation, California.

The initial phases of this study were funded by the University of Utah Research Fund, Salt Lake City.

TABLE OF CONTENTS

10   Background

13   I   Santa Fe to El Vado

21   II   Ute Country: Puerta Grande to the La Plata River

33   III   Mesa Verde and the Land of the Anasazis

45   IV   Red Rock Country: Piute Spring to the Green River Desert

55   V   Green River Crossing, San Rafael Country, and Castle Valley

61   VI   Salina Canyon, Sevier River, and the Fish Lake Route

67   VII   Circleville to Mountain Meadows

75 VIII   The Virgin River: Utah, Arizona, Nevada

85   IX   California Crossing, Las Vegas, and Spring Mountains

97   X   The Mojave Desert

111   XI   Barstow, Mojave River, and the Approach to Cajon Pass

119   XII   Los Angeles: Cajon Pass to the Plaza

127   Bibliography

137   Map Bibliography

141   Index

BACKGROUND

Spain, you will recall, following the discoveries of Columbus, overran the Americas with amazing speed. Coronado's men reached the south rim of the Grand Canyon within fifty years after Columbus' first landfall. Colonization followed exploration. Juan de Oñate planted a settlement in New Mexico in 1598. Later settlements, like the fingers of a hand, were made in Texas and California, as if Spain were reaching northward to take hold of the continent. As Spain was challenged in North America by European powers, she attempted to fill in the gaps between these fingers of settlement.

One such move was directed by two Franciscan friars, Francisco Atanasio Domínguez and Francisco Silvestre Vélez de Escalante, who in 1776 hoped to open a route between Santa Fe and Monterey in California. They did not achieve this objective, but they did pass through and describe for the first time the interior regions, now part of Colorado, Utah, Arizona, and New Mexico. The expedition is well documented. The friars crossed some areas later followed by the Spanish Trail, though these places were limited to sections in Colorado and New Mexico.

We want to emphasize that the Domínguez-Escalante Trail is not coterminous with the Spanish Trail, except in a few places. A third Franciscan, Francisco Tomas Hermenegildo Garcés, also in 1776, attempted to find a route between California and New Mexico. But he too failed in his objective. Garcés explored a segment of the Spanish Trail along the Mojave River in California.

In 1776, Spain's power in the New World began to fade, and her possessions in North America were lost to revolutionaries who created independent Mexico in 1821. While Spain had closed the doors to international commerce in her possessions in North America, Mexico opened them. Thus, commercial traffic over the Santa Fe Trail between the United States and New Mexico began in 1822.

California ports were also opened to international traffic. The commencement of trade between the Mexican provinces of New Mexico and California was stimulated by this new, international outlook. New Mexico was sheep country, and had been so as a Spanish colony. Wool and woven textiles, which had been major items of trade between New Mexico and the older settlements, now became principal items in the trade between New Mexico and California, which prospered under a booming international commerce. Horses and mules, abundant in pastoral California, found a ready market in New Mexico, while cattle formed the basis in California for a sea-borne commerce in hides and tallow.

Not long after Lewis and Clark, American and British fur men roamed the interior wildernesses of the Rocky Mountains and Great Basin in pursuit of beaver. The American fur men hunted the northern reaches of Mexico and frequently visited the outlying settlements at Taos, Santa Fe, and San Gabriel. The American trapper, Jedediah Smith, bridging the gap between the tracks of Domínguez-Escalante and Garcés, in 1826 and again in 1827, was the first to travel overland from the mountain interior to California.

With the quickening of international life, the Spanish Trail was opened in 1829-1831. The Mexican, Antonio Armijo, in 1829, was the first to carry commercial goods from New Mexico to California over portions of what was to become the Spanish Trail. Two Americans, William Wolfskill and George C. Yount, journeyed over the general route of the Spanish Trail in the winter of 1830-1831. Thereafter, the trail as we have described it here became the major thoroughfare between the provinces of New Mexico and California.

The Spanish Trail was a horse and mule trail, not a wagon road. Goods were transported on the backs of mules. Pack trains, as much as a mile in length, were kept in line by packers and drivers. Merchants from New Mexico, carrying raw wool and locally woven textiles, would leave in the fall before winter snows set in. Generally, the return trip was made in the early spring to avoid the high water in the Green and Colorado rivers. Each way, the trip took about two and one-half months to complete. Herds of up to two thousand animals or more were driven from California to New Mexico. By 1841, the overland trade was well organized and subject to government regulations.

Along the way, the traders sometimes took slaves from the Paiute Indians living in Utah, Arizona, and Nevada, and these were sold in New Mexico and California. In addition to the wool merchants, American traders and trappers, Indians, and New Mexican settlers moving to California, used the trail.

Of course, the Spanish Trail was not Spanish. It was opened and used during the Mexican period and should be appropriately named the Mexican Trail. American explorers, when retracing sections of the trail, assumed that it had been opened by Spain and consequently misnamed it.

By running northward as far as Green River, Utah, the trail riders avoided the great canyons of the Colorado River, and the hostile tribes on the more direct line through Arizona. In 1848, Mexico lost the region now crossed by the Spanish Trail to the United States; and overland commerce, thereafter, followed direct east-west lines. The Spanish Trail, as we have delineated it here, soon ceased to exist as a trade route.

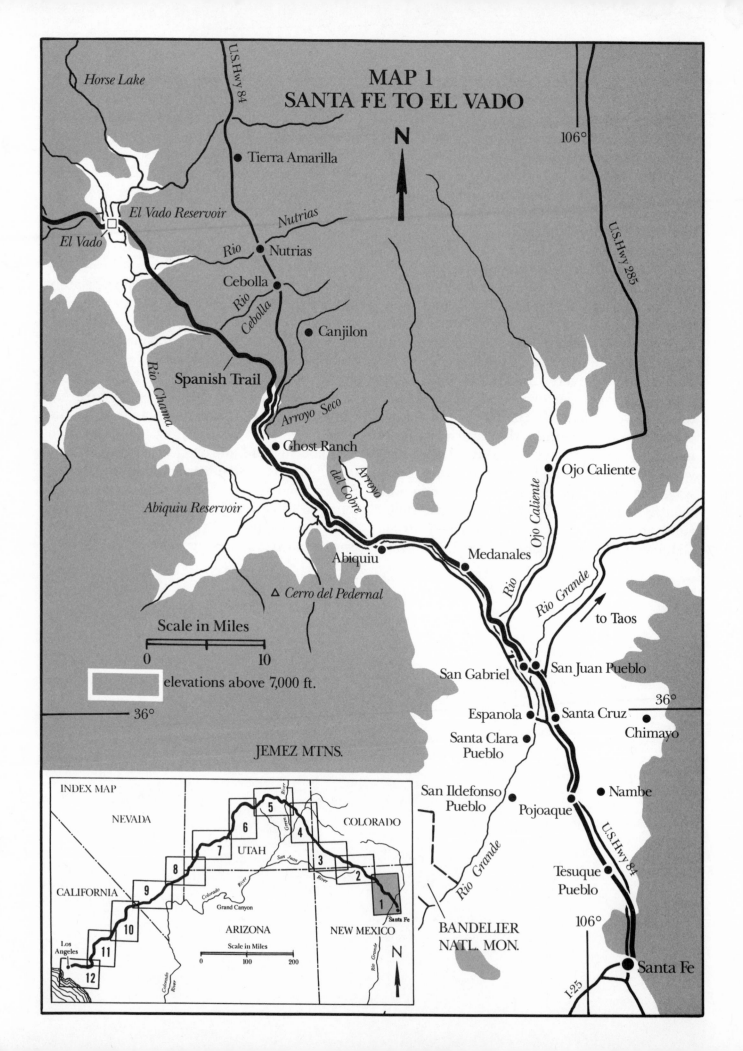

MAP 1
SANTA FE TO EL VADO

N

Horse Lake

U.S.Hwy 84

Tierra Amarilla

106°

El Vado Reservoir

Nutrias

El Vado

Rio Nutrias

Cebolla

Rio Cebolla

Canjilon

U.S.Hwy 285

Spanish Trail

Rio Chama

Arroyo Seco

Ghost Ranch

Arroyo del Cobre

Ojo Caliente

Abiquiu Reservoir

Ojo Caliente

Medanales

Rio Ojo Caliente

Rio Grande

△ Cerro del Pedernal

to Taos

Scale in Miles

0   10

San Gabriel

San Juan Pueblo

elevations above 7,000 ft.

Espanola

Santa Cruz

36°

36°

Santa Clara Pueblo

Chimayo

JEMEZ MTNS.

San Ildefonso Pueblo

Nambe

Pojoaque

INDEX MAP

River

NEVADA

5

COLORADO

Green River

6

4

San Juan

Rio Grande

San Ildefonso Pueblo

7

UTAH

3

Nambe

8

San Juan River

2

Pojoaque

9

Colorado River

Grand Canyon

1

U.S.Hwy 84

CALIFORNIA

Santa Fe

Tesuque Pueblo

10

ARIZONA

NEW MEXICO

BANDELIER NATL. MON.

106°

Los Angeles

11

Scale in Miles

0   100   200

12

Colorado River

Rio Grande

N

I-25

Santa Fe

TOP LEFT: *Tourists shopping for American Indian crafts on the arcade of the Palace of the Governors.*

LEFT: *Interior courtyard of the Palace of the Governors.*

ABOVE: *Santa Fe Museum of Fine Arts, adjacent to the Palace.*

CHAPTER I

SANTA FE TO EL VADO

Caravans heading to California started from the plaza of the ancient city of Santa Fe and advanced northward up the valley of the Rio Grande. They followed well-traveled roads, which carried them through Spanish and Indian settlements to the frontier outpost of Abiquiu on the Rio Chama, a historic gateway to the Colorado Plateau. Northwest of Abiquiu, the trail crossed the Rio Chama at El Vado, a ford first described by the Domínguez-Escalante Expedition in 1776.

SANTA FE

Founded by Spain in 1610, Santa Fe was a typical Spanish-Mexican town with government buildings, commercial establishments, and some private dwellings located around a central plaza.[1] The traders from Missouri wheeled their wagons onto the plaza to conduct their business, and traders bound for California started from the same place. If you were to walk around the plaza today, it would be easy to imagine the excitement as animals,

[1] *Much has been written about the Spanish history of New Mexico, including the Spanish missionary system. Adams and Chavez (1956) is the report on visits to the New Mexican missions carried out by Domínguez in 1776. We note that the expedition headed by Domínguez and Escalante was an outgrowth of the Domínguez visitation. A study by Kessell (1980) examines the history of the New Mexican missions after 1776, during the time when they were most visited by travelers on the Spanish Trail.*

LEFT: *California-bound caravans passed in front of this church at Santa Cruz.* La Villa Nueva de Santa Cruz de la Cañada *was the second formal municipality established in present-day New Mexico. It was founded by Diego de Vargas in 1695 in the fertile Española Valley.*

ABOVE: *San Ildefonso Pueblo.*

laden with packs, emerged from adjacent neighborhoods to form a train ready to leave the capital city.

Step into the governor's quarters (the "Palace"), a museum today, to view graphic illustrations of New Mexico's history. Visit the gift shop for a fine selection of books and publications of regional importance. Sample the museum's journal, *El Palacio,* devoted to New Mexico's rich cultural history. Serious students of the Spanish Trail will want to visit the library, also located in the palace, to start an investigation of the historic route. Here we found several of the rarer books that were used in our study of the trail.

SANTA FE TO ABIQUIU

Between Santa Fe and Abiquiu on the Rio Chama, traders bound for California, 1829-1848, followed roads developed by Indians centuries before the coming of the white men. One road, on the west side of the Rio Grande, ran up to the Chama through San Ildefonso Pueblo, Santa Clara Pueblo, and Española. On the east side of the Rio Grande Valley, a main road ran through Tesuque Pueblo, Pojoaque, Santa Cruz, and San Juan Pueblo, at the confluence of the Rio Grande and the Rio Chama. From San Juan, a major road continued on to Taos Pueblo. From Taos, a trail, sometimes called the northern branch of the Spanish Trail, reached Grand Junction, Colorado, and joined the main Spanish Trail at a point just east of Green River, Utah.

Spanish history at San Juan goes back to 1598 when Juan de Oñate, at the head of a large colonizing expedition, arrived at San Juan, where he founded the first Spanish settlement in New Mexico. The colonists took up residence in a suburb of the pueblo on the

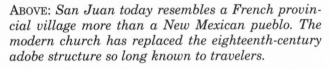

ABOVE: *San Juan today resembles a French provincial village more than a New Mexican pueblo. The modern church has replaced the eighteenth-century adobe structure so long known to travelers.*

TOP RIGHT: *Site of San Gabriel, first Spanish settlement in New Mexico, founded in 1598 by Juan de Oñate.*

RIGHT: *Along the Rio Chama near Medanales, a colonial and modern weaving center.*

west side of the Rio Grande, which Oñate named San Gabriel. This was the "capital" of New Mexico until 1610 when Santa Fe was named the seat of government. Thereafter, San Gabriel was left to molder, and by the 1830s and 1840s, when the California caravans passed directly through the place, very few remains of the original settlement were visible. Excavating the site in recent years, archaeologists have revealed the outlines of the "lost" San Gabriel and found that the native village had been a flourishing pueblo dating back to about A.D. 1250.[2]

Heading in the mountains on the New Mexico-Colorado boundary, and draining the eastern slope of the continental divide, the Rio Chama flows south and southwest to reach the Rio Grande, just below the San Juan Pueblo. The valley of the Chama was a natural and historic gateway from the Rio Grande to the Colorado Plateau much used by prehistoric and modern Indian peoples, Spanish explorers, fur trappers, California-bound traders, prospectors, and by U.S. Army expeditions, federal surveyors, and Indian agents.[3]

ABIQUIU

From the Rio Grande, the California traders rode up along the bottom lands of the Rio Chama to the frontier outpost of Abiquiu, founded by the Spanish government in 1754, in part, as a settlement for *genizaros*—Indians of diverse tribal origins who had adopted Spanish ways of living. By design, Abiquiu

[2] When Cultures Meet *(1987) describes the history of the archaeological investigations at Spanish San Gabriel.*

[3] Swadesh *(1974) examines the advance of the frontier up the Chama River Valley.*

was a buffer against marauding Indians—Utes among them—coming from the north-west. In times of peace, a fair was held here in the early fall when the Utes came to trade dressed deerskins for Spanish horses. [4]

Rich in history and a picturesque place on a hill overlooking the Chama Valley, Abiquiu, before 1848, was the last white settlement on the Spanish Trail between New Mexico and the frontier outliers in California, a distance of well over a thousand miles. This was a rendezvous and real starting point for many travelers and caravans heading out on the long trail. Since the country above Santa Fe was fully known, Charles Dimmock, diarist and cartographer of the Macomb military expedition, 1859, deemed it "superfluous" to start his diary before leaving Abiquiu. Dimmock was much taken with the "magical variety of outline and shape" of the rock for-

mations around Abiquiu. To see them, he thought that "every traveller through that strange region" would be compelled "to wander awhile from the beaten trail."[5]

One who later found inspirational beauty

---

[4] *Kessell (1980) provides details on the founding and subsequent history of Abiquiu.*

[5] *We have few eye witness accounts of travelers on the Spanish Trail. One of our best diarists is Charles Dimmock, diarist and cartographer of the expedition to the confluence of the Green and Grand (Colorado) rivers, headed by Captain John N. Macomb in 1859. Macomb (1876) is the basic published document of the expedition. Dimmock mapped the route, mile by mile, and his unpublished diary (1859) is laden with observations about places on the trail. Dimmock's manuscript map is in the National Archives. The map, accompanying the official report of the expedition, based on Dimmock's manuscript map, was drawn by F. W. Egloffstein, who issued the map separately under his own name in 1864.*

Rocky segments of the Spanish Trail, six miles west of Abiquiu.

in the region was Georgia O'Keeffe, nationally famous painter who lived in Abiquiu for forty-one years before her death in 1986.[6]

California-bound travelers had a choice of well-established roads between Santa Fe and Abiquiu. Beyond that point, the choices narrowed. For most of the way there was a single track or, in places, a series of parallel tracks. We plan to follow these tracks—the Spanish Trail—all the way to California. Charles Dimmock, member of the Macomb exploring expedition following the Spanish Trail, will be our guide through parts of New Mexico, Colorado, and Utah.

GHOST RANCH

At six miles from Abiquiu, the trail leaves the Chama over a difficult, rocky stretch and, crossing some open, rolling country, reaches Arroyo Seco, a Chama tributary emptying into the Abiquiu reservoir. Following up the arroyo, there are multi-colored cliffs on the right where paleontologists have found the last resting place of assorted dinosaurs, including Coelophysis, the "little dinosaur" of the Triassic.

Ghost Ranch, a 21,000-acre spread on a tributary of the Arroyo Seco, a stone's throw from the Spanish Trail, is a national conference center of the Presbyterian Church, where seminars on many subjects are offered without distinction of creed or racial origin. On the grounds of Ghost Ranch, at the Florence Hawley Ellis Museum of Anthropology, exhibits describe the history of the three cultural groups in New Mexico—Indian, Spanish, and Anglo. On the highway near the

---

[6] *Lisle (1986) is a recent biography. Since O'Keeffe's death, numerous articles on her life and painting have been published.*

LEFT: Cerro del Pedernal, *also known as Abiquiu Peak, a towering landmark above the Chama River Valley, was visible from the Spanish Trail. From a sketch by J. S. Newberry, geologist with the Macomb military expedition, 1859.*
MACOMB, REPORT, 1876.

RIGHT: *Negative copy of a section of the original Dimmock map, 1859, showing the route of the Macomb Expedition from Arroyo Seco to the Rio Nutria[s], via [Rio] Cebolla. Note that the "Old Spanish Trail" departs from the Macomb Trail near the Rio Cebolla. The map clearly indicates campsites and the mile-by-mile measurement of the Macomb route.*
NATIONAL ARCHIVES

entrance to the ranch, is the Ghost Ranch Living Museum, dedicated to regional ecology and conservation.[7]

RIO CEBOLLA AND RIO NUTRIAS

Twelve miles beyond Ghost Ranch, we followed the Spanish Trail as it left the Arroyo Seco, turned up Navajo Canyon, and then, as Charles Dimmock writes, crossed a "gently undulating sage plain" to the Rio Cebolla. Here, in 1859, the Macomb expedition left the Spanish Trail and headed north to Pagosa Springs and Piedra Parada, generally following the route of the Domínguez-Escalante expedition of 1776. We will meet both of these parties again at the Animas River.[8]

Beyond Rio Cebolla, we traced the Spanish Trail through open country, watered by the Rio Nutrias, to El Vado on the Rio Chama.

EL VADO TO PUERTA GRANDE

El Vado (the ford) on the Rio Chama, first appears on the maps made by Bernardo Miera y Pacheco, cartographer for the expedition led by Francisco Atanasio Domínguez and Francisco Silvestre Veléz de Escalante. In their historic quest for a suitable trail between New Mexico and California, Domínguez and Escalante crossed the river here on August 3, 1776.

After studying the Escalante diary, the

---

[7] *Pack (1979), who founded the ranch and donated it to the Presbyterian Church, writes of the Spanish-Mexican-Indian tradition about ghosts in the earliest local Spanish settlements. Ellis (n.d.) has written a summary of twelve centuries of the history of northern New Mexico.*

[8] *Macomb was aware that he had left the Spanish Trail at the Rio Cebolla as Dimmock mentions in his diary.*

LEFT: *El Vado Reservoir now covers the historic Domínguez-Escalante and Spanish Trail crossing of the Chama River.*

BELOW LEFT: *Ghost Ranch looking south to the landmark peak, Pedernal.*

BELOW: *Puerta Grande on the Spanish Trail west of El Vado Reservoir.*

Miera map, and the terrain, we conclude that the 1776 expedition and the Spanish Trail crossed the Chama at very nearly the same place. This was close to a turn-of-the-century lumbering camp, named El Vado, now covered by the El Vado Reservoir, a state park. El Vado Lake Resort is a recreational facility on the dam's eastern side.

Beyond El Vado, Escalante mentioned that there were three large mesas running from north to south, separated by two gaps, beyond which there were two lakes. He named the three mesas "Los Santisima Trinidad," (The Most Holy Trinity). It is obvious to us, from an on-the-ground survey, that the Spanish Trail passed through the southernmost gap, which now bears the name "Puerta Grande" (wide gateway), to reach,

after eight easy miles, Lago Hediondo (Stinking Lake or Burford Lake in modern times).[9]

---

[9] *Although the Domínguez-Escalante expedition carried out an important exploration of the interiors of New Mexico, Colorado, Utah, and Arizona, it did not complete its basic objective. The diary of the expedition, usually attributed to Escalante, has been edited by Herbert E. Bolton (1950), by Warner and Chavez (1976), and by other students. The Bolton edition contains a facsimile copy of Miera's map of the expedition's travels, issued in 1778. A unique facsimile of the Miera map was published by Yale University in 1970 from an original in its collection. Our interpretation of El Vado is at variance with the Domínguez-Escalante trail survey done under the auspices of the Four Corners Regional Commission, a study edited by David E. Miller (1976).*

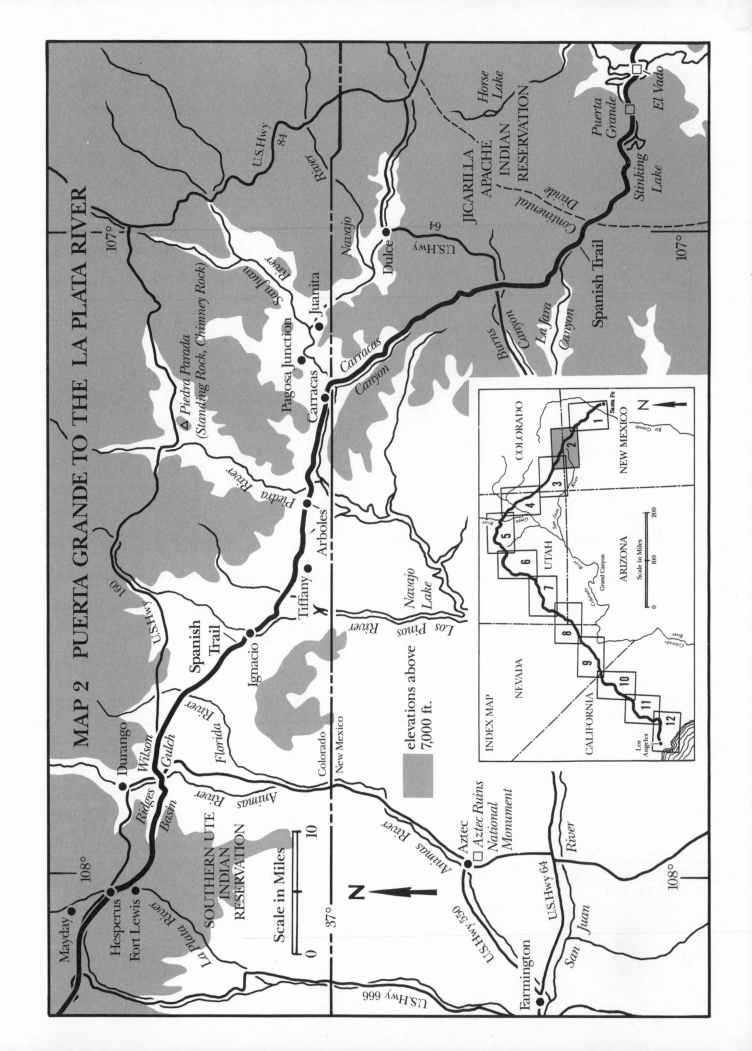

MAP 2 PUERTA GRANDE TO THE LA PLATA RIVER

Section of Atlas Sheet No. 69 issued by the Wheeler Survey in 1882. The trail passes through the breaks in two parallel igneous dikes—the Dike Rock Ridge[s] on the Geological Survey map. Burford Lake (Hediondo L.) appears on the lower right corner of the map. The Denver & Rio Grande Railroad is shown at Carracas. The Jicarilla Apache Reservation was not created until 1887.

CHAPTER II

UTE COUNTRY: PUERTA GRANDE TO THE LA PLATA RIVER

From El Vado, the Spanish Trail passes through an open gateway between two mesas, called Puerta Grande, before continuing over the Continental Divide separating the waters of the Rio Grande and the Colorado. Between Carracas and the La Plata River, the trail crosses the several headwaters of the San Juan River, a region long dominated by the Ute Indians. The Spanish Trail crossing of the Animas River, near Durango, was a ford used by the earliest explorers of the region.

JICARILLA APACHE INDIAN RESERVATION

Circling around the north shore of Lago Hediondo, the Spanish Trail, heading northwest across the Jicarilla Apache Indian Reservation, eases over the Continental Divide at an elevation of approximately 7,600 feet above sea level, at about 36°40' north latitude.

The Jicarilla reservation, created in 1887, is generally open, wooded, rough, and with few distinguishing focal points or landmarks. From the divide, we determined that the Spanish Trail continued on a northwesterly course across the reservation, and the adjoining Carson National Forest, to reach the San Juan River through Carracas Canyon.

We were helped here by studying Atlas Sheet No. 69, issued by the Wheeler Survey in 1882. This beautiful hachured map, scale eight miles to the inch, covers a block of

Spanish Trail crossing of the San Juan River at Carracas.

territory from Santa Fe on the southeast to Durango and Fort Lewis on the northwest.[1] Wheeler shows the "Old Spanish Trail," from "Hediondo L." to Carracas on the San Juan River, passing through the breaks in two parallel igneous dikes—the Dike Rock Ridge[s] on the local Geological Survey topographic map.

Even with the Wheeler map and modern topographic maps, we found it difficult to trace the Spanish Trail from Burford Lake to the head of Carracas Canyon. Through much of this distance, numbers of secondary roads seemed to go nowhere, and the few paved roads ran in the wrong directions. At one time, a now impassable wagon road followed the Spanish Trail in Carracas Canyon. The Jicarilla tribal government at Dulce, where there is a fine museum, and the forest service ranger staff at Gobernador, New Mexico,

provided us with maps and information. After studying this material and some other sources, and after jeeping-about a great deal over terrain that seemingly had seen little through-traffic since Spanish Trail days, we feel confident about the accuracy of the route as we have laid it down on the accompanying map.

Carracas, by way of the Spanish Trail, is

[1] *Map, Wheeler (1882). Along with Clarence King, John W. Powell, and Ferdinand V. Hayden, George M. Wheeler headed up one of the Great Surveys of the West following the Civil War. Coming under U.S. Army jurisdiction, Wheeler set out to prepare an atlas of the West, suitable for military purposes. Before his survey was disbanded in 1879, Wheeler had mapped much of the territory covered by the Spanish Trail from Santa Fe to Los Angeles. His atlas sheets are still useful and constitute documents of primary historical interest.*

Pagosa Junction, on the D&RG near Carracas, is a museum of a place where a section of track, a bridge, and a false front are reminders of the railroad days.

140.645 miles from Santa Fe.[2] Here, where there was once a station on the Denver and Rio Grande Railroad, and where a small settlement remains, the Spanish Trail reached and crossed the San Juan River. This is a place of special beauty. The clear waters of the San Juan flow quietly along over gravel bars, between low banks, shaded by groves of cottonwoods.

SAN JUAN RIVER

At the Continental Divide, the traveler on the Spanish Trail enters the basin of the San Juan River, a part of the vast Colorado Plateau, a region rich in history and containing over two dozen national parks and monuments, protecting spectacular archaeological and geological features. Since the old trail passes near so many of these reserves, as well as a number of state parks, it might well be called the "Trail to the Parks."

Beyond Carracas, the Spanish Trail follows the north bank of the San Juan, crosses the tributary Piedra River near Arboles, and then angles off to the northwest. Navajo Lake, the reservoir created by Navajo Dam, a federal reclamation project, covers much of the trail below Carracas and the Piedra crossing. The visitor center near Arboles at Navajo State Recreation Area, a Colorado state park, features interpretive exhibits on regional history from prehistoric to modern times. One panel shows the course of the Spanish Trail through the reservoir area.

---

[2] *The Denver & Rio Grande Railroad, building westward, reached Carracas in 1880 and, thence, continued the line on to Ignacio and Durango and to Dolores (1892). See Myrick (1970)* New Mexico's Railroads.

Marker at the Navajo State Recreation Area near Arboles describes the Domínguez-Escalante expedition that passed through this region in 1776.

UTE COUNTRY—IGNACIO

Beyond Arboles, we traced the Spanish Trail across open, rolling country dotted by many small ranches and fields, outlined by low hills, covered with piñon, juniper, oak, and sagebrush. The trail passes through Ignacio on Los Pinos River, once a station on the D&RG, now agency headquarters of the Southern Ute Indian Reservation.[3]

The Ute Indians, whose lands were penetrated by the Spanish Trail, once lived and roamed over central and western Colorado, and eastern and central Utah. In organized bands, they moved about on foot, living on fish and game, and wild plants. With the coming of the Spaniards to New Mexico, the Indians' way of life changed dramatically, as they acquired Spanish horses and a variety of European tools and weapons. Three bands bordering the Spanish settlements on the north were the first of the Utes to benefit from the horse and the other cultural riches imported by Spain. Reading from the east to west, these were the Muache, Capote, and Weminuche bands, which, together, appear in the literature as the Southern Utes. The Pueblo Revolt in 1680 provided a major opportunity for the tribes to rustle the stock left behind by the Spaniards, and the Southern Utes made the most of it. Already equestrians by 1680, the Southern Utes now increased their herds and, therefore, their power in dealing with friend or enemy.

After the Pueblo Revolt, the aboriginal use of horses—passing from tribe to tribe—

[3] *For a scholarly tri-ethnic study of the upper Chama and the Ute frontier of the San Juan, see Swadesh (1974). A basic reference on the Ute Indians is the* Handbook of North American Indians, *volume 11, Warren L. D'Azevedo, ed., (1986).*

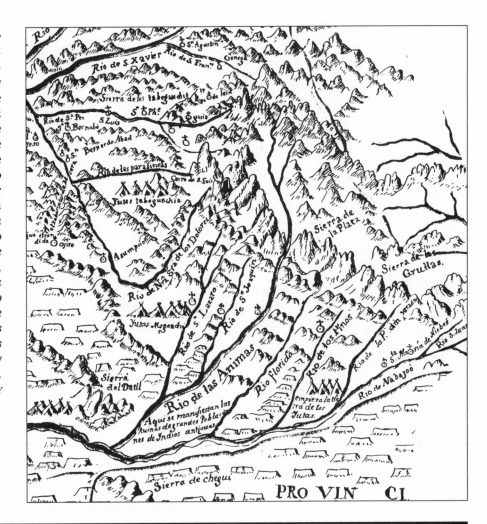

Section of map made by Bernardo de Miera, cartographer of the Domínguez-Escalante expedition, showing the explorers' route from the "Rio S. Juan" to "Rio de Nra Sra de los Dolores." The Spanish Trail followed the Domínguez-Escalante route from the San Juan River to the Dolores River. Translated: Rio de Nabajoo (San Juan River), Rio de la Piedra Parada (Piedra River), Rio Florida (Florida River), Rio de las Animas (Animas River), Rio de San Joaquin (La Plata River), Rio de San Lazaro (Mancos River), and Rio de Nra Sra de los Dolores (Dolores River). Campsites along the route are shown by the circle and cross symbol.
<small>UTAH STATE HISTORICAL SOCIETY</small>

spread from the New Mexico base. West of the Rockies, the migration of horses, furthered by the Ute bands of southwestern Colorado, reached the tribes of the Northwest within a few years. Thus, when Lewis and Clark crossed the continent, 1804-1806, they found that the Shoshoni Indians in Montana were riding Spanish horses.[4] The migration route to the northwest quite probably followed the route of the Spanish Trail through southwestern Colorado to Moab, and to Green River, Utah, where it branched off to the Great Salt Lake and regions beyond.

Before the advent of the Spanish Trail, in the latter part of the eighteenth century, the easing of relations between the Spaniards and the Utes (Yutas to the Spaniards) opened the way for the explorations of Juan Maria Antonio de Rivera, Domínguez and Escalante. Early in the nineteenth century,

at least two trading parties from New Mexico had reached the Ute Indians living on the shores of Utah Lake in north central Utah.[5] And, during the Mexican period, trappers and traders, ranging through Ute country, and travelers on the Spanish Trail, 1829-1848, were seldom molested. In 1848, by the treaty of Guadalupe-Hidalgo, ending the war with Mexico, the United States acquired all of what we call the Southwest, and this included all of the Ute lands. Within a few years, the Utes found themselves in the path of the westering American miners, railroad builders, settlers, and stockmen. The Indians agreed to accept life on reservations. The Southern Utes were assigned a narrow

---

[4] *Roe (1955) traces the spread of the horse northward from New Mexico and other Spanish border areas.*
[5] *Hill (1930), 16-19.*

strip of land in southwestern Colorado.

Riding horseback for well over a hundred and fifty years before 1848, and following the age-old footpaths of the Anasazi Indians who came before them, the Southern Utes opened the San Juan country to equestrian traffic. The white men who entered their country, and pushed them aside, most certainly followed the Indians' main traveled trails, one of which became the route we now call the Spanish Trail.

In Ignacio, travelers following the Spanish Trail should visit the Southern Ute Cultural Center (convention facility, lodge, restaurant, lounge, gallery, and museum) on the north edge of town. The museum displays clearly indicate the importance of the horse in Ute history.

CROSSING OF THE ANIMAS

From Ignacio, we followed the Spanish Trail for about 13 miles across open rolling country to the Animas River, about four and one half miles downstream from the city of Durango. We found that the Spanish Trail reaches the Animas through Wilson Gulch, a natural eastern gateway to the river, which here flows through a narrow valley, bordered by steep banks. This was a historic crossing point of the Rio Animas. It was probably here, on July 4, 1765, that Juan Maria Antonio de Rivera, heading up Spain's first ever *entrada* to the San Juan country, reached the river and named it the Rio de las Animas. Eleven years later, on August 8, 1776, the Domínguez-Escalante expedition reached this same point.[6]

---

[6] *The long lost diaries of the Rivera expeditions, carried out in 1765, have been translated and edited by Austin N. Leiby (1984). The Domínguez-Escalante entrada is described by Bolton (1950).*

The Spanish Trail crosses here. Orville Pratt, en route to California, forded the river here on September 8, 1848. The Macomb expedition, which had left the Spanish Trail back at the Rio Cebolla, rejoined it here on the Animas in August 1859. Expedition members wrote that the river, its waters clear, deep, rapid, and "fish abounding," was not easily forded.[7]

Once across the river, directly opposite the mouth of Wilson Gulch, travelers were forced to climb a steep gravel and boulder terrace, three hundred feet high. Escalante described the trail: "We left the Rio de las Animas, climbed the west bank of the river which, although it is not very high, is quite difficult because it is very stony and in places very rugged."

We found traces of the old trail, now grown over with brush and trees, running up the steep slope at an angle. It was quite obvious that it had not been used for many years. We were able to follow the trail by looking for rust stains on the gravel and boulders. Rust stains?[8] When shod animals, climbing the

---

[7] *Pratt (1954), 347; Dimmock (1859); and Macomb (1876), 80.*

[8] *To determine the metallic content of the rust stains, the authors submitted samples of the stained rocks to Dr. Max P. Erickson of the University of Utah Department of Geology and Geophysics, and to the Utah Engineering Experiment Station, a scientific laboratory on the University of Utah campus. Dr. Erickson, using a binocular microscope, found metallic iron by scraping off a thin surface layer of the stain. The malleable, underlying material was attracted to a hand magnet. He concluded that the markings "represented rust from iron abraded from horseshoes." The scientific lab, using x-ray flourescence, found deposits of iron on the rocks that had been produced by "striking or rubbing the surface of the rock by iron horse-shoes."*

ABOVE: *The Animas River at the Spanish Trail crossing. A suburb of the City of Durango appears in the background.*

OPPOSITE PAGE: *The Spanish Trail ascends the steep terrace on the western side of the Animas River. Shod horses slipped on water-worn rocks, leaving a thin coat of iron which soon turned to rust.*

steep slope, slipped on the hard, rounded rocks, a thin layer of iron was deposited on them. As the slip marks oxidized, they appeared as rust-colored streaks on the light-colored rocks. Thus, we could follow this "trail of rust" from the base to the top of the terrace, a distance of a quarter of a mile. There are only a few such "rusty places." The Spanish Trail was a dirt trail. Where it crossed rocky places, most of the rocks were soft, and rust stains soon eroded away. Though short, the trail up from the Animas was one of the steepest places on the Spanish Trail. It was never developed later as a wagon road.

DURANGO

During the frantic railroad building era after the Civil War, the rails followed the trails in many places in the American West. In order to get to the developing mines in the San Juan Mountains of Colorado, the Denver and Rio Grande Railroad reached Carracas in 1880. West of that point, the railroad generally followed the Spanish Trail. Building over the old trail down through Wilson Gulch to the Animas, the D&RG avoided the steep Spanish Trail across the river, turned north, and laid out the town of Durango opposite the mouth of Lightner Canyon, a natural gateway to the west.

In a frontier environment, Durango prospered from the start, and it is one of the largest cities adjacent to the Spanish Trail. We visited the Center of Southwest Studies at Fort Lewis College, in Durango, and found it to be rich in materials covering regional history from prehistoric to modern times. We urge travelers on the Spanish Trail to stop and sample the abundant materials in the Center.[9]

RIO DE LA PLATA

From the terrace top above the Animas, using Dimmock's notes, we followed the Spanish Trail as it passes through Ridges Basin and a sparsely wooded, open country, to the La Plata River. The trail reaches the La Plata near Ute Junction, once a station on the D&RG Railroad, some two miles above Fort Lewis, a U.S. Army post established in 1880.

Beyond Ute Junction, the Spanish Trail swings northward, and for two miles, follows up the La Plata River flowing from the towering La Plata Mountains straight ahead. The river was "one of the loveliest streams I think I ever saw," wrote Orville Pratt on September 8, 1848.[10] Eleven years later, the Macomb expedition camped along this reach, August 5, 1859. The beauty of the site so charmed geologist J. S. Newberry that he filled a page in his diary:

...the Rio de la Plata is a beautifully clear, cold, mountain-brook...well-stocked with trout. The valley in which it flows, as it issues from the mountains, is exceedingly beautiful, and our camp, one of the most delightful imaginable. Our tents are pitched in the shade of a cluster of gigantic pines, such as are scattered, here and there, singly or in groups, over the surface of the valley, separated by meadows thickly coated with the finest gramma grass. Stretching off southward, a wall of verdure, tinted with the fresh and vivid green of cottonwoods and willows, marks, while it conceals, the course of the sparkling stream whose murmuring flow comes softly to the ear. On either side of the valley rise picturesque wooded hills, which

[9] *Robert W. Delaney, former director of the center, prepared a guide indexing the holdings of the institution, suitable for serious research. Delaney, comp. (1979).*
[10] *Pratt (1954), 347.*

ABOVE: *Close-up of iron-stained rock from the Las Animas terrace.*

LEFT: *Hesperus on the Spanish Trail.*

OPPOSITE PAGE: *Here, on the divide between the LaPlata River and Cherry Creek, the Spanish Trail reached an elevation of 8330 feet.*

bound the view both east and west; between these on the south an open vista reveals, far in the distance, the blue chains of the Sierra del Carriso and Tunecha [Carrizo and Chuska mountains]. On the north the bold and lofty summits of the Sierra de la Plata look down upon us in this pure atmosphere with an apparent proximity almost startling.

Descriptions of the landscape like this are rare in the early literature of the frontier West. Although the Spanish Trail passes through some of the grandest scenic places in the Southwest, one looks in vain for any considerable appreciation of the landscape until the twentieth century. Most of the travelers along the trail were not touched by the scenery; they just ignored it. Lawyer Orville Pratt and geologist Newberry were passing through forested mountains along one of the highest sections of the entire caravan route.[11]

At Hesperus, two miles beyond Ute Junction, the Spanish Trail turns westward to cross the divide between the La Plata and one of its lengthy tributaries, Cherry Creek, where the elevation is about 8,330 feet. The cool mountain green was a respected prospect to the mid-century American, and our travelers responded to it with sincere enthusiasm. West beyond this section, where the trail passes through the arid lands and harsh desert regions, landscape appreciation is seldom found in the literature. Near the Cherry Creek divide, and about two miles above Hesperus, John Moss, prospector, adventurer, explorer, in 1873, with a

[11] *Newberry in Macomb (1876), 81. Newberry, who wrote most of the Macomb report, gives us some of the best descriptions of the Spanish Trail between New Mexico and Utah. Both Orville Pratt (1954) and Newberry had a fine eye for natural scenery.*

company of California miners, discovered coarse gold in the gravel bars along the La Plata. When the news got out, eager prospectors following the Spanish Trail rushed in from east and west, and a sprawling collection of tents and wickiups sprouted on Gold Bar along the river. Remembering the San Francisco banking firm which had grubstaked the venture, Moss named the camp Parrott City. When richer diggings were found elsewhere in the San Juan Mountains, the "Parrott" became a ghost.[12]

---

[12] *Map, Hayden (1877), Sheet IX, shows the location of Parrott City at the head of Gold Bar, a few miles north of the "Old Spanish Trail," which is depicted from Carracas Canyon to Dove Creek, and beyond. Sheet VIII of this beautiful atlas shows the "Old Spanish Trail" running from the Great Sage Plain to and through the La Sal Mountains. "Spanish Valley," the site of the soon-to-develop Moab, is also shown.*

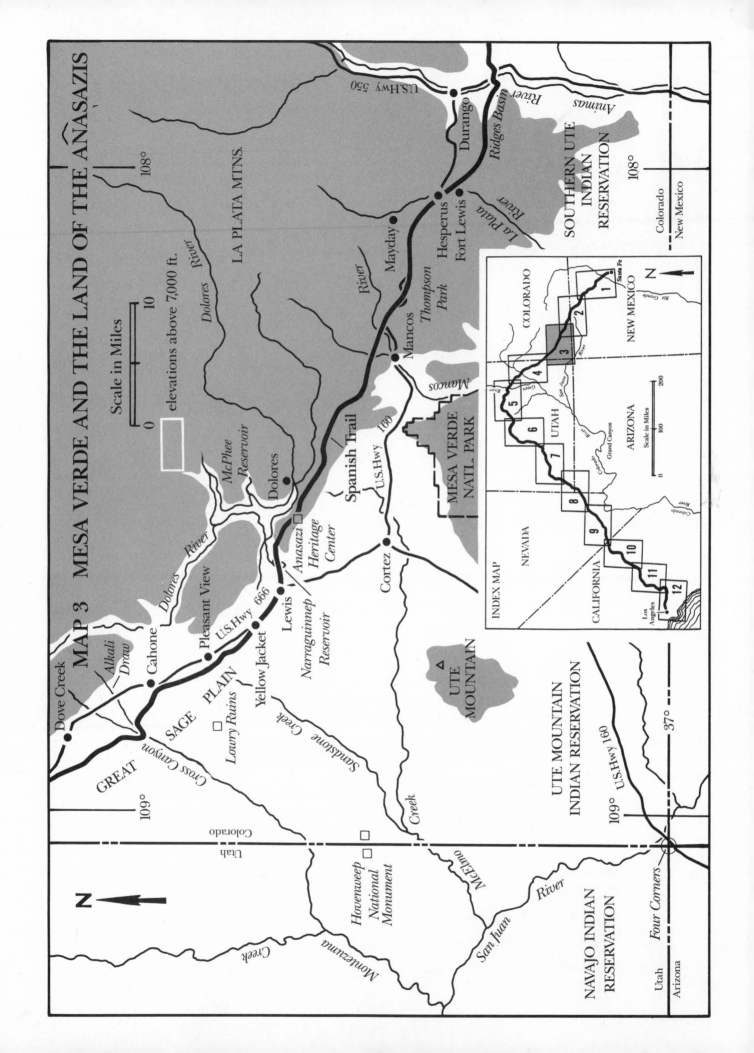

MAP 3   MESA VERDE AND THE LAND OF THE AÑASAZIS

LEFT: *The Spanish Trail passed through the center of Thompson Park.*

BELOW: *Main Street, Dolores, Colorado.*

CHAPTER III

MESA VERDE AND THE LAND OF THE ANASAZIS

Leaving the La Plata region, the Spanish Trail passes through the territory of the great prehistoric Anasazis who, for well over a thousand years, lived in towns and villages built on the mesas and the open country drained by tributaries of the San Juan River. Travelers on the trail encountered some of the ruins of their imposing settlements. But the great ruins at Mesa Verde, adjacent to the trail, were not seen by white men until the 1870s. Beyond Mesa Verde, the Spanish Trail crosses an extensive open area, named by geologist Newberry in 1859, the "Great Sage Plain."

LA PLATA—MANCOS PASSAGE

West of the La Plata-Cherry Creek divide, the Spanish Trail closely followed Cherry Creek, dropping down over grassy swales and narrow meadows to Thompson Park. From the highway along this stretch, we could see what appeared to be sections of the old trail where it crosses low, hummocky places near the creek. Thompson Park is a high mountain valley, grassy-floored and surrounded by the wooded slopes of the San Juan National Forest. Crossing a low pass at the west end of the park, the trail descends (clearly visible high on the west side of the pass) to the open valley of the Mancos River. Two miles above the town of Mancos, a settlement of farmers and ranchers dating from the early 1870s, the Spanish Trail crosses the main forks of the Mancos River and continues on over an open valley, dotted with

Galloping Goose No. 5 in downtown Dolores.

The Rio Grande Southern Hotel at Dolores is a reminder of the town's railroad history.

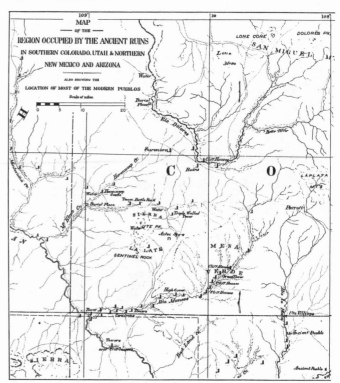
Map published in 1878 by the Hayden Survey shows explorations of 1874-1876 by William H. Jackson and William H. Holmes who discovered many historic sites, but did not find the Anasazi ruins on Mesa Verde. The ruins shown in Mesa Verde are those discovered by Jackson in Mancos Canyon, which descends to the south of the national park.

groves of piñon and juniper, to Dolores.

The passage between the La Plata and Mancos rivers is one of the places in the San Juan region where all those following the Spanish Trail traveled the same path. Here, for a few miles, was a single track. Elsewhere in many places, the Spanish Trail is less well defined. There were alternate routes, cut-offs, short cuts, diversions and detours. Here, the great trading caravans operating between New Mexico and California followed a way opened by prehistoric Indians, mounted Ute Indians, eighteenth century Spanish explorers, as well as Rocky Mountain fur trappers and traders. Only a few years after the last of the caravans had gone, American frontiersmen, government explorers, rushers after gold and silver mines, cattle drovers, road and railroad builders, in succession, passed this way. And now, U.S. 160, a major federal highway crossing southern Colorado, traverses the La Plata-Mancos passage.

DOLORES

The Dolores River, an important point on the Spanish Trail, is a maverick stream. Heading high in the San Miguel Mountains, it flows southwestward for about 50 miles. Then, instead of continuing on this course and joining the San Juan River, it abruptly swings around to the northwest, creating a big bend, and flows in that direction to reach the Colorado River about 100 miles distant.

The recorded history of the Dolores dates back to 1765, when Juan Maria Antonio de Rivera, from New Mexico, reached the river in July, and again in October. It appears likely that Rivera gave us the name: Nuestra Señora de los Dolores—"Our Lady of Sorrows."[1]

[1] *Leiby (1984).*

Cliff Palace, Mesa Verde.

On their trek westward, Domínguez and Escalante reached the Big Bend of the Dolores where they camped, August 12-13, 1776. This would be a good place for a settlement, Escalante wrote in his diary. There were "irrigable lands, pasture, timber and firewood." People had lived here in "ancient times," Escalante observed. On an elevation on the south bank of the river, the two padres examined some ruins of a "small settlement" similar in form to the villages of New Mexican Indians.[2]

On August 10, 1859, the Macomb expedition reached this point where Domínguez and Escalante had camped eighty-three years earlier. Geologist Newberry, whose words illuminate so many places along the Spanish Trail, describes the Dolores at the Big Bend: "A clear, rapid stream" running "through a beautiful but narrow valley... the bottom-lands are nearly level, half a mile wide, and very fertile, covered with fine grass, with groves of cottonwood and willow, and scattered trees of yellow pine. Near the river the thickets are overgrown with virgin's bower and hop, which form impenetrable jungles. Great numbers of flowers ornament the grounds...."

Newberry also viewed the ruins visited by Domínguez and Escalante. A hill on the south side of the river

is crowned with an extensive series of very ancient ruins. The principal one is a pueblo, nearly 100 feet square, once substantially built of dressed stone, now a shapeless heap. . . .Like most of the ruined pueblos of New Mexico, it consisted of a series of small rooms clustered together, like cells in a beehive. Near the principal edifice are mounds of stone, representing subordinate buildings. Among these are

<hr>

[2] *Bolton (1950), 141.*

Anasazi Heritage Center complex. The prehistoric Dominguez Ruin appears at lower left. The Escalante Ruin can be seen at top center. J. FLEETMAN, BUREAU OF RECLAMATION

numerous large depressions marking the places of cisterns or *estuffas* (kivas). Quantities of broken pottery, similar to that so commonly seen in like circumstances, but bearing the marks of great age, strew the ground about these ruins.

A mile or two up the river, Newberry saw the ruins of several small stone houses built on ledges under projecting rocks. They were occupied, he surmised, "by the guardians of the fields" who once cultivated lands along the river bottom.[3]

That the Big Bend of the Dolores was an important stopping place on the Spanish Trail is suggested by the writings of Escalante and Newberry who were describing, for the first time, the prehistoric ruins of the Anasazi people in the Mesa Verde region. Somewhere near the present town of Dolores, one can easily picture a great caravan spread out in camp (away from the thickets covered with virgin's bower and hop!) along the shaded, grassy bottoms of the river.

Today's Dolores was first a railroad town on the narrow-gauge Rio Grande Southern, which early in 1892 began running trains connecting Durango, Mancos, Dolores (the rails between these points, in places, paralleled the Spanish Trail) and the high mountain mining districts to the north. As the frontier of settlement moved out to the big country toward the west—Newberry's Great Sage Plain—Dolores became the nearest rail head and shipping point for settlements as far away as Monticello in southeastern Utah. The main traveled road for horsemen, wagons, stages, livestock drovers—often called the Monticello Road—was practically identical with the Spanish Trail.

---

[3] *Newberry in Macomb (1876), 86, 88.*

36

ABOVE: *The Wetherills' Alamo Ranch at Mancos, Colorado.*

ABOVE RIGHT: *Main entrance, Anasazi Heritage Center.*

RIGHT: *Escalante Ruin at the Anasazi Heritage Center. The craggy mass of Mesa Verde appears in the distance.*

The Great Depression crippled the Rio Grande Southern and, in 1931, regular train service to Dolores was suspended. Well, not entirely. A gasoline-powered, automobile rail-bus contraption was devised to continue service. Carrying a few passengers, mail and freight, these vehicles—each called a "galloping goose" from the way it seemed to waddle and wobble down the track—lasted until 1951. Goose No. 5 is retired and may be seen on the grounds of the Dolores town hall. Plans for its restoration are being developed by the Galloping Goose Historical Society.

MESA VERDE NATIONAL PARK

Many of the millions who travel to see the ancient Anasazi ruins at Mesa Verde National Park are following sections of the Spanish Trail. The prehistoric Anasazi people occupied much of the Four Corners region.

They lived by farming, although they did engage in hunting. As farmers, they became rooted to the soil and gradually developed hamlets, villages and, eventually, large apartment houses, including many imposing cliff dwellings, typified by those in Mesa Verde National Park. For reasons not fully understood, some time before A.D. 1300 the Anasazi abandoned their homeland in the Four Corners, and their great urban centers at Mesa Verde and elsewhere became the first ghost towns in the Southwest. Some distance from the Spanish Trail, the Anasazi remains on Mesa Verde were not discovered until the 1870s.

J. S. Newberry's description of the ancient ruins at Dolores was one of the first notices of the Anasazi cultures in Colorado to reach the general public. Before leaving the Big Bend of the Dolores, Newberry had

ABOVE: *Ute Mountain, a distinguishing landmark in the heart of Four Corners country.*

RIGHT: *Sheep in pasture at Lewis, Colorado, on the Spanish Trail.*

hiked to the top of one of the ramparts of Mesa Verde. He wanted to see the country off to the west, which he named the "Great Sage Plain," where the expedition was headed. Newberry did not reach the celebrated ruins of the park, but it is quite probable that the name, Mesa Verde, dates from the time of the Macomb expedition, since we find it first named on the Dimmock map (1859) and copied on the Egloffstein map of 1864. The Egloffstein map appeared at a time when rumors were flying about that undiscovered ruins of ancient cities, possibly of Aztec origin, existed in southwestern Colorado.

Ferdinand V. Hayden, director of the United States Geographical and Geological Survey of the Territories, sent two of his best men to investigate. During the years 1874, 1875, and 1876, reconnaissance parties headed by artist-photographer William H. Jackson, and artist-topographer-geologist-anthropologist William H. Holmes discovered and described many of the ancient Anasazi ruins in southwestern Colorado and southeastern Utah. In September 1874, the first party in the field, headed by Jackson and guided by John Moss of Parrott City, passed through Mancos Valley and on into Mancos Canyon, where Jackson found and photographed and sketched cliff dwellings, towers, and other ruins. Beyond Mancos Canyon, the Jackson party made a wide swing to the west, recording ancient sites on McElmo, Hovenweep, and Montezuma creeks.

During the years they were in the field, the men of the Hayden Survey worked all around the craggy mass of the Mesa Verde, but they did not explore the maze of canyons

LEFT: *Yellow Jacket, Colorado.*

BELOW: *Archaeologists from the University of Colorado have been excavating at Yellow Jacket for over 30 years. Ute Mountain appears in the background.*

draining the elevated plateau.[4] It remained for the Wetherill family, based at their Alamo Ranch near Mancos, to reveal to the world the dramatic Anasazi remains of Mesa Verde.

With abundant grazing and farm lands, Mancos developed as a supply point for the mining districts of the La Plata high country. Benjamin and Marion Wetherill, and their five sons, established their ranch there, and with the permission of the Ute Indians, ranged cattle down into Mancos Canyon. In December 1888, Richard Wetherill and brother-in-law Charles Mason were looking for some stray cows on the elevated slopes of Mesa Verde when they happened upon the spectacular, pre-Columbian, Anasazi ruins at Cliff Palace and Spruce Tree House. Within a short time, the Wetherills and their associates, ranging through its intricate canyon system, had discovered most of the major ruins of the Mesa Verde.

The news of these discoveries brought many visitors who came to see the cliff dwellings. Most of them stayed at the Alamo Ranch and were guided to the ruins by the Wetherills. The published works of two early visitors helped to create a national and international interest in Mesa Verde. F. H. Chapin's popular account, *Land of the Cliff Dwellers*, appeared in 1892, followed in 1893 by *The Cliff Dwellers of the Mesa Verde*, an elaborate study made by a young Swedish scientist and traveler, Gustaf Nordenskiold. By the end of

[4] *Hayden, along with Powell, Wheeler, and King, directed one of the Great Surveys of the West, 1867-1878. Some of Hayden's most notable work was done in Colorado, where he mapped the topography and geology of the state, the results of which were published in his famous atlas (1877). Jackson's reports were contained in the* Annual Reports *of the Hayden Survey. Jackson's reconnaissance of 1874 appeared in the* Eighth Annual Report *(1876).*

ABOVE: *A section of the sprawling Anasazi ruins at Yellow Jacket. These are culturally similar to those at Mesa Verde. Ute Mountain in the distance.*

LEFT: *Spanish Trail in Alkali Draw, the eastern approach to Cross Canyon. Dr. Newberry of the Macomb Expedition wrote of the "monotonous flat Sage Plain."*

the century, Mesa Verde had become the best known archaeological zone in the United States. National park status came in 1906. In 1978, the United Nations Educational, Scientific, and Cultural Organization selected Mesa Verde National Park as a world heritage cultural site. Exhibits at the Far View Visitor Center and the Chapin Mesa Museum place the park in historical perspective.[5]

ANASAZI HERITAGE CENTER

West of Dolores, near the spot where Domínguez and Escalante in 1776, and Newberry in 1859, noted the ancient ruins, and directly on the Spanish Trail, there now stands the imposing Anasazi Heritage Center. Opened in 1989, it is a major museum and research facility, dedicated to the study and interpretation of the prehistoric cultures in the Four Corners region. Operated by the

Bureau of Land Management, the center staff manages about two million artifacts, most of which came from the Dolores Archaeological Salvage Project which preceded the building of McPhee Dam on the Dolores River. The center, open to the public, houses laboratories, a library and theater, a gift and book shop, and extensive interpretive exhibits.

CORTEZ AND MONTEZUMA

From the Anasazi Heritage Center, five miles north of Cortez, the Spanish Trail continues its course through Montezuma County. No, neither Cortés nor Montezuma slept here. Some of the early American visitors to south-

---

[5] *There is an abundant literature on Mesa Verde, its prehistoric inhabitants, and their culture. Robert and Florence Lister (1983) summarize the cultural history of Mesa Verde and other southwestern parks and monuments.*

There is no traffic now through Cross Canyon, and cliff swallows have taken up residence at the register rock near the historic springs.

western Colorado imagined that the many prehistoric ruins which they saw were left by migrating Aztecs moving into Mexico. On some of the early maps, including township surveys, we see reference to "Aztec towers," etc. Thus, when Colorado created a new county, what better name than Montezuma, and when the county seat was established, what better name than Cortez?

Reclamation on the Dolores River brought Cortez into existence in 1887, and the recently completed, massive Dolores Project has strengthened the city's position as the economic hub of the region.

Visitors to this part of the Southwest will encounter the phrase "Four Corners," which is applied to the region centering at the point where the boundaries of Colorado, New Mexico, Arizona, and Utah come together. The region may extend outward as far as a hun-

dred miles from the center, depending on the objectives of the user of the term. For example, we may say that the Spanish Trail, from the La Plata River to the Abajo Mountains, passed through the Four Corners country.[6]

YELLOW JACKET

Within the Four Corners, the Anasazi country extended west beyond Dolores and Mesa Verde, across the Great Sage Plain to Dove Creek and eastern Utah. The Spanish Trail passes through or near some of the more important prehistoric sites along the way. Using the map of our old friend, Charles Dimmock, we were able to trace the trail for some 13 miles through the Narraguinnep Reservoir and Lewis, to Yellow Jacket Ruin, located at the head of Yellow Jacket Canyon. Here, the Spanish Trail passes by an open

[6] *Vandenbusche and Smith (1981).*

41

Cut stone structure in Cross Canyon, said to have been the headquarters of the Carlisle Cattle Company.

field of several acres filled with crumbling Anasazi ruins, first described in 1859 by Dr. Newberry of the Macomb expedition. Judging by the remains of large stone houses, pottery fragments and milling stones, reservoirs and canals, he thought that "several thousand" people may have lived here. Newberry learned that the ruined town was named Surouaro, a Ute word signifying desolation. An appropriate word, he wrote, since the "surrounding country is hopelessly sterile; and, whatever it once may have been, Surouaro is now desolate enough."

Newberry's Surouaro is now Yellow Jacket Ruin, a nationally important prehistoric site excavated and studied by archaeologists from the University of Colorado Museum for over thirty years. The large number of kivas, or ceremonial rooms, found at the site suggest that Yellow Jacket was an Anasazi ceremonial center with an estimated population of 1,500-

3,000 persons. Inquire at the Colorado University Center and Museum in central Cortez for information about on-going excavations and tours. Exhibits at the museum illustrate the rich fabric of the region's prehistoric life.[7]

CROSS CANYON

Traveling along the Spanish Trail across the Great Sage Plain beyond Dolores, the Macomb party saw no flowing streams at all, only springs. One of these, wrote Newberry, was at Tierra Blanca (White Place), now Cross Canyon, where the water issued from the base of a low sandstone cliff whitened by mineral salts. We have determined that the Spanish Trail reaches Tierra Blanca by way of Alkali Draw, a Cross Canyon tributary.

Cross Canyon was a regular stop on the

[7] *Lange, et. al., (1986) is a booklet descriptive of the history and archaeology of the Yellow Jacket Ruin. Newberry in Macomb (1876), 88.*

RIGHT: *Dry farming near Dove Creek and elsewhere on the Sage Plain has obliterated most traces of the Spanish Trail.*

BELOW: *Dove Creek's proclamation.*

Dolores-Monticello Road, which followed the Spanish Trail, and it appears to have been a major watering place for cattle drovers moving animals from Texas on to the ranges on the Abajo and La Sal Mountains in southeastern Utah in the late 1870s.

There is no through-traffic now. The modern highway by-passes the springs. With the decline of traffic through Cross Canyon, cliff swallows have taken up residence at a pioneer register rock near the historic springs.

Leaving Cross Canyon, we followed the Spanish Trail on a northwesterly course crossing the head of Monument Creek, two miles west of the town of Dove Creek.

DOVE CREEK

Dove Creek is in the center of a large agricultural area, once heavily occupied by the dry-farming Anasazi Indians. The American settlers moving into the region in the 1920s also practiced dry farming and found that the soil and climate were ideally suited to the growing of beans, winter wheat, sunflowers, and dry land alfalfa. The Chamber of Commerce proudly proclaims that Dove Creek is the "Pinto Bean Capital of the World." Many of the bean fields are planted in the same areas the Indians farmed, and today's growers say that pieces of pottery and arrowheads come off their bean cleaners regularly. Owing to the intensity of farming, the Spanish Trail cannot be directly followed through this area, and we must rely on the maps of Dimmock and F. W. von Egloffstein, supplemented by the original plats of township surveys, which show the "Old road to Monticello, Utah to Dolores." We know that the Monticello Road generally followed the Spanish Trail and, thus, we can map the trail with some accuracy from the vicinity of Dove Creek to the Utah border.

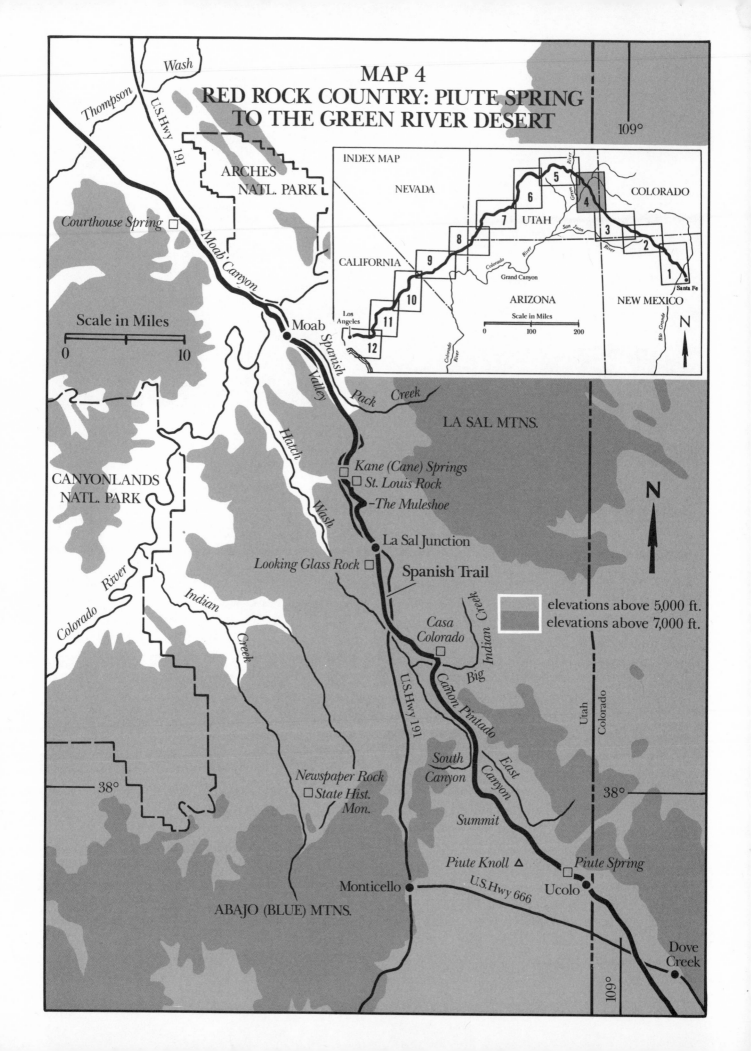

MAP 4
RED ROCK COUNTRY: PIUTE SPRING TO THE GREEN RIVER DESERT

109°

Thompson *Wash*

U.S.Hwy 191

ARCHES NATL. PARK

Courthouse Spring □

Moab Canyon

Moab

Spanish Valley

Pack Creek

LA SAL MTNS.

Hatch Wash

INDEX MAP

NEVADA

5
6
7
8
9
10
11
12

UTAH

CALIFORNIA

COLORADO

4
3
2
1

Santa Fe

Grand Canyon

ARIZONA

NEW MEXICO

Los Angeles

Green River
San Juan River
Colorado River
Rio Grande

Scale in Miles
0   100   200

N

Scale in Miles
0   10

CANYONLANDS NATL. PARK

Colorado River

Indian Creek

Kane (Cane) Springs □
□ St. Louis Rock
—The Muleshoe

La Sal Junction

Looking Glass Rock □

Spanish Trail

Casa Colorado □

Big Indian Creek

elevations above 5,000 ft.
elevations above 7,000 ft.

N

U.S.Hwy 191

Cañon Pintado

East Canyon

South Canyon

Newspaper Rock
□ State Hist. Mon.

Summit

38°

38°

Utah
Colorado

Piute Knoll △

Piute Spring □

Monticello ●

U.S.Hwy 666

Ucolo

ABAJO (BLUE) MTNS.

109°

Dove Creek ●

ABOVE: *The "pour-off" at Ucolo below Piute Spring.*

ABOVE RIGHT: *A section of the "Monticello Road"-Spanish Trail in Colorado near the Utah border.*

RIGHT: *The ranch at Piute Spring, a major watering hole on the Spanish Trail.*

CHAPTER IV

RED ROCK COUNTRY: PIUTE SPRING TO THE GREEN RIVER DESERT

Taking a northwesterly course beyond Piute Spring and the Summit area of the Great Sage Plain, the Spanish Trail penetrates a section of the spectacular, red rock canyon country of the Colorado River. Trail riders were afforded extraordinary views of the sculptured formations adjacent to Canyonlands and Arches national parks. Riders reached the Green River Desert after fording the Colorado River at Moab and passing through the colorful Moab Canyon. The two isolated mountain masses of the Abajo and La Sal Mountains were landmarks for all travelers on the trail.

PIUTE SPRING

The Spanish Trail crosses the Colorado-Utah border at mile 269.840 from Santa Fe.

Two miles beyond the border is Piute Spring. With a steady flow of good water, it was a most important stopping place on the Spanish Trail. Here, the Carlisle Cattle Company established a headquarters in the 1870s. A military reconnaissance from Fort Lewis, Colorado, under Lieutenant E. H. Ruffner, stopped at "Ute" Spring on October 7, 1878.[1] Another command from the same post was based here for a time in 1884. It was a major camp site on the Monticello-Dolores road from the 1890s. The area was homesteaded by H. U. Butt of Monticello in 1912. The Butt family was part of a frontier movement carried out largely by Utah Mormons who moved eastward from Monticello, at the base

---
[1] *Map, Humphrey (1878).*

45

ABOVE LEFT: *The Abajo Mountains, an important landmark visible from the trail, were known to Spanish explorers as early as 1776. The Abajos are known locally as the Blue Mountains or "the Blues."* PARKER HAMILTON

ABOVE RIGHT: *Beyond Piute Spring, a section of the Spanish Trail has escaped the plow.*

BELOW: *Part of a panorama drawn by W. H. Holmes for the Hayden Survey showing the region between the Sage Plain and the La Sal Mountains. Holmes uses letters to identify places. "O" identifies Cañon Pintado (East Canyon); "L" is Casa Colorado; "J" is the La Sal Mountains.* HAYDEN SURVEY, ANNUAL REPORT, 1878.

of the Abajo Mountains, to take up lands for dry farming along the Utah-Colorado border.

Just beyond the Utah border, the Spanish Trail passes a point known today as Ucolo. Here, the overflow from Piute Spring runs down Piute Draw to a spillway, known locally as the "Pour-off." We believe that this is the place identified on the Dimmock map as Guajolote (salamander). Dimmock says that Guajolote is a "canyon slimy with water-lizards."[2]

The Spanish Trail continues up Piute Draw to Piute Spring, and on across Dimmock's "interminable sage plain," to the Summit area, the extreme northwestern part of the Great Sage Plain plateau, drained in the main by the headstreams of East Canyon, a tributary of the Colorado River.

CAÑON PINTADO

From the Summit area, the Spanish Trail by way of South Canyon drops down a thousand feet to the nearly level floor of East Canyon, a nine-mile-long gash in the northwestern corner of the Sage Plain plateau. With great difficulty, we located the South Canyon route, assisted by information supplied by local ranchers. Orville Pratt wrote of this section on September 13, 1848: "…We began descending one of the longest & steepest mountains yet passed over. But we got down it with safety. After reaching the bottom the scenery in the valley was the most rugged & sublime I ever beheld."[3] The Macomb party reached this same location, and geologist Newberry, who had a fine eye for scenic, as well as geological landscape, found delights in the brilliant

---

[2] *Dimmock (1859), and map, Dimmock (1859).*
[3] *Pratt (1954), 348.*

46

ABOVE LEFT: *Casa Colorado.*

LEFT: *Casa Colorado, a striking landmark of red sandstone along the Spanish Trail. The La Sal Mountains loom in the background. From a sketch by J. S. Newberry of the Macomb expedition, 1859.* MACOMB, REPORT, *1876.*

ABOVE: *The tanks (Las Tinajas) at the base of Casa Colorado formed an important watering place on the trail.*

coloring of the canyon walls, "the lower half composed of strata which are bright red, green, yellow, or white." The brilliant coloring suggested the name Cañon Pintado (Painted Canyon), a name which, unhappily, never got far beyond the pages of Newberry's "Geological Report."[4] His fine geological eye led him to the discovery of some Sauropod bones in the canyon walls of Cañon Pintado. The Sauropod site has recently been rediscovered by F. A. Barnes, writer-photographer of Moab, Utah, and studies to determine its scientific significance are under way by paleontologists.[5]

CASA COLORADO

From the mouth of East Canyon, or Cañon Pintado, the Spanish Trail crosses open Dry Valley, a drab name for a great basin hollowed out of predominantly red rock. Drained by Hatch Wash, and stretching away north and west toward the Colorado River, it has been a winter range since the early 1880s, when the big cattle outfits first came into southeastern Utah. About seven miles from its camp in Cañon Pintado, the Macomb party reached La Tinaja (The Tank), located near the slickrock base of Casa Colorado (Red House). The name, Casa Colorado, appears first in Newberry's geological report, and his sketch of the rock was published in that report. The name was later adopted by the Hayden Survey. This prominent landmark, a striking red sandstone rock rising two hundred feet above an elevated base, was so-named because its several sculptured caves and alcoves resembled the windows of a giant house.

---

[4] *Newberry in Macomb (1876), 90.*

[5] *Barnes (1989), 16.*

47

Section of petro-glyph panel at Newspaper Rock State Historical Monument shows mounted Indians hunting.

Newberry found La Tinaja to be a "deep excavation in red sandstone, which retains so large a quantity of surface water and for so long a time, as to become an important watering place on the Spanish Trail." In a region typified by Dry Valley, where one seldom finds living, running water, these natural rock reservoirs, taking the forms of tanks, potholes, basins, and cavities, were a boon to desert travelers, providing them water for drinking and even bathing.

Archaeological evidence near Casa Colorado reflects heavy use by both prehistoric Indians and modern tribes, particularly by the Utes. The Spanish Trail in Dry Valley passes near many prehistoric sites, some of which, as seen in panels of petroglyphs, show evidence of modern Indian cultures. The outstanding panel at Newspaper Rock State Historical Monument, west of the Spanish Trail and near Canyonlands National Park, portrays modern Indians on horseback.

About six miles beyond Casa Colorado, the Macomb expedition left the Spanish Trail and went on to Ojo Verde, where camp was set up as a base for further explorations. Looking for the confluence of the Colorado and Green rivers, the explorers were probably the first white men to enter what is now the Needles section of Canyonlands National Park.[6]

From Casa Colorado, we traced the Spanish Trail, which followed a northwesterly course, past Looking Glass Rock, a lone

---

[6] *Newberry in Macomb (1876) describes the Spanish Trail from Casa Colorado to Ojo Verde. Barnes (1989) carries the explorers from Ojo Verde to Canyonlands National Park. For a study of the rock art in Newspaper Rock State Historical Monument, see Castleton (1979).*

ABOVE: *Dry Valley. The infrequent storms replenish the desert watering holes.*

ABOVE RIGHT: *A modern range camp in Dry Valley near the Spanish Trail.*

RIGHT: *Looking Glass Rock, seen by riders on the Spanish Trail.*

monument over a hundred feet high, perforated by a natural window, and on to Kane Springs at the base of the bold St. Louis Rock. In later years, stockmen herding cattle along the sandstone bluffs on this section of the Spanish Trail reported that it was one of the hottest places on the drive, where animals' tongues distended as they hastened to reach the springs.

KANE SPRINGS

These bountiful springs at the foot of St. Louis Rock have served travelers since Spanish Trail days. The rock may have been named during those days, but we have found no record of it before 1855, when a Mormon exploring expedition, passing along the trail at this point, used the name St. Louis Rock. The names of many travelers are written or chiseled on the rock, but they postdate 1855.[7]

The State of Utah maintains a highway rest stop here. The dark green of trees and lawn stand out in pleasant contrast to the red rock of the promontory towering 1,300 feet above the historic site.

Leaving the springs behind, travelers on the Spanish Trail followed a narrow, rocky trail, which brought them out to the head of Spanish Valley. We were able to identify the trail in this section with little difficulty.

MOAB

Within a distance of 14 miles, the trail passes through Spanish and Moab valleys (actually one continuous valley) to reach the Colorado River northwest of the city of Moab. This is one of the most scenic places along the trail. A steep wall of red rock,

[7] *Madsen (1991), 25.*

49

ABOVE: *Roadside tourist attraction occupies the lower part of St. Louis Rock.*

ABOVE RIGHT: *The narrow, rocky section of the trail near Kane Springs. Vehicles shown are on adjacent highway.*

RIGHT: *Trail riders on Kane Springs Wash would see this view of the La Sal Mountains, known to Spanish explorers as early as 1776.*

1,500 feet high, flanks the valley on the southwest, but the opposite wall is much lower, permitting views of the laccolithic peaks of the La Sal Mountains, towering over 12,000 feet on the southeastern skyline, some 15 miles distant.

The level valley floor, about two miles wide, was easy going; and travelers on the trail found good grass and pure water in Pack Creek and Mill Creek, which head in the La Sals and flow through the valley (confluent below Moab) to the Colorado River. During the trail days, Pack Creek was called Salt Creek, or Little Salt Creek, a name derived from the La Sal (Salt) Mountains, not from a salty taste.

Right on the Spanish Trail, a county seat, a bustling trade center and tourist capital, Moab was founded in 1855 as the Elk Mountain Mission by the Church of Jesus Christ of Latter-day Saints. In that same year, when Ute Indians killed three of the missionaries, the Mormons pulled out. Permanent settlers did not return until the 1870s. Thereafter, Moab became a supply point for much of southeastern Utah and adjoining sections of Colorado. Traffic through the region passes over sections of the Spanish Trail, a fact known to early settlers who may have given it the name Spanish Valley.[8] The name first appears in print in the Atlas of the Hayden Survey published in 1877.[9]

The archaeology, history, and natural history of the Colorado Plateau in southeastern Utah and the Four Corners region is nicely displayed in the galleries of the Dan O'Laurie Museum in the center of town. *Canyon*

[8] *Tanner (1976).*

[9] *Map, Hayden Atlas (1877).*

ABOVE: *An example of the many spectacular rock formations along the Colorado River near Moab.*

ABOVE RIGHT: *Moab Main Street as it appeared in the 1920s.* DAN O'LAURIE MUSEUM

RIGHT: *Spanish Trail crossing of the Colorado River at Moab.*

Legacy, the museum's impressive quarterly, touches on subjects as diverse as movie making, dinosaurs, and river history.

CROSSING OF THE COLORADO RIVER

C. S. Cecil Thomson of Moab, long a prominent figure in the history of regional transportation, located for us sections of the trail from Dry Valley to points across the Colorado River north of Moab. According to local tradition, he said, the trail passed directly through the city to the crossing of the Colorado River. Probable location? About half a mile downstream from the present highway bridge. There the river is about two hundred fifty yards wide, but an island appears at low water and the bottom is firm. Fording would have been possible at lowest water; however, most travelers, like Orville Pratt in 1848, found it necessary to swim the animals across the river and raft the

goods and equipment.[10] The northwest bank of the crossing lay between the uranium mill and the mouth of Courthouse Wash. Beyond the river, the trail went up Moab Canyon past the entrance to Arches National Park.

ARCHES NATIONAL PARK

A short distance from the Colorado River, the entrance to Arches National Park is right on the Spanish Trail. The Park is well named. Nearly ninety stone arches, windows, and openings have been discovered here amid a spectacular array of cliffs, spires, alcoves, fins, and balanced rocks. Although nine miles away, some of the stone windows in the park could have been seen by riders at some points on the Spanish Trail. It seems likely that trappers following the Spanish Trail, heading for the upper Green River country, might well

[10] *Pratt (1954), 348-349.*

51

The Spanish Trail was used by trappers heading to the upper Green River country from New Mexico. This inscription by Antoine Robidoux is located in Westwater Canyon, some distance north and east of Arches National Park and east of the Spanish Trail.

have passed through Arches National Park.[11]

Today's travelers following the trail will profit from the exhibits in the visitor center at the Park's entrance. Displays feature geology, natural history, and archaeology. There is also a well-stocked bookshop. The visitor center here also serves Canyonlands National Park.

TO THE GUNNISON TRAIL

Beyond Arches, the Spanish Trail continues up Moab Canyon, enclosed by spectacular, deep red cliffs and slopes for several miles. At 11 miles from Arches, the trail reaches Courthouse Spring, probably Upper Courthouse Spring on modern maps, described by Orville Pratt as a "small, run of living water." Now on a northwest beeline course, we followed the trail through open, barren desert country to Little Grand Wash. Here, our trail

research was helped along by the report of John W. Gunnison, captain in the Army Corps of Topographical Engineers, who had been commissioned by the War Department in 1853 to undertake a railroad survey across the West along the 38th and 39th parallels of latitude, the "central route." Antoine Leroux, the old mountain man who guided the surveyors through the Colorado Rockies, told them that near the Green River they would reach the Spanish Trail, which "is broad, well marked and easy to follow."[12] The Gunnison train, which included nineteen supply wagons, reached the trail near Little Grand Wash on September 29, 1853, and for the next three weeks, with some detours, the explorers followed it all the way to the Sevier River where

---

[11] *Hoffman (1985), 57-58.*

[12] *Parkhill (1965), 170.*

ABOVE LEFT: *Modern highway covers the Spanish Trail near the entrance to Arches National Park.*

ABOVE: *The plentiful grass and water at Upper Courthouse Spring.* S. K. MADSEN

LEFT: *Open, barren desert near the Gunnison Trail.*

Gunnison and some members of his party were killed by Indians.[13] With the Gunnison report and maps in hand, we followed the Spanish Trail across Green River, the San Rafael Swell, and the Wasatch Plateau.

[13] *Beckwith (1855).*

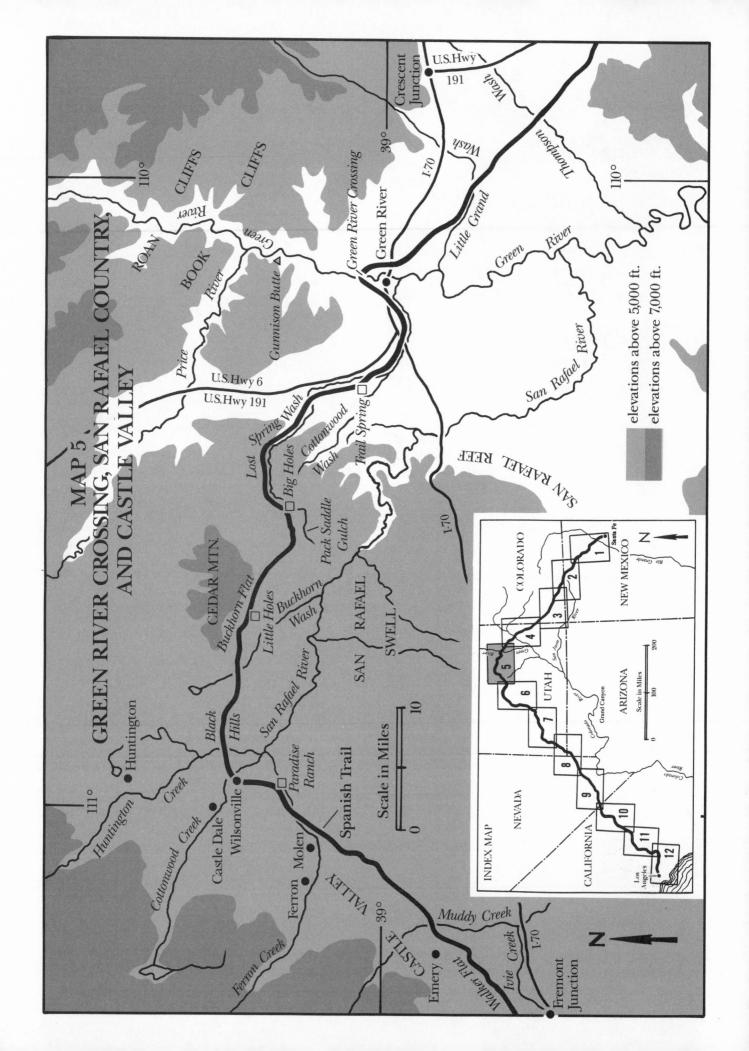

MAP 5,
GREEN RIVER CROSSING, SAN RAFAEL COUNTRY, AND CASTLE VALLEY

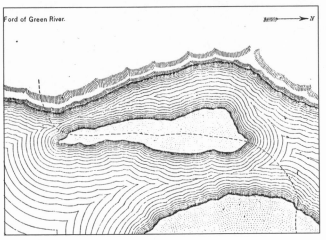

Ford of Green River.

LEFT: *The modes of travel across the Green River provide a mini-history. First came the Spanish Trail, a ford. Later, a ferry was operated here. Then came the D&RG Railroad, and later the highway bridged the stream, all near Green River City.*

LEFT BELOW: *Detail of the Spanish Trail crossing of the Green River published by the Hayden Survey, 1877. On the sketch, the river flows from right to left.* HAYDEN SURVEY, NINTH ANNUAL REPORT, 1877

BELOW: *Pioneer waterwheel above the Spanish Trail crossing on the Green River. The Book Cliffs form the skyline.* S. K. MADSEN

CHAPTER V

GREEN RIVER CROSSING, SAN RAFAEL COUNTRY, AND CASTLE VALLEY

In the desert country at the base of the Book Cliffs, the Spanish Trail crosses the Green River, an important crossroads in post-trail days. Beyond the river, the trail passes through the rugged northern reaches of the deeply eroded San Rafael Swell, before it turns south into Castle Valley, settled by pioneer Mormons in the 1870s.

GREEN RIVER CROSSING

After reaching the Spanish Trail, near the base of the Book Cliffs on the Green River Desert, the Gunnison railroad survey party traveled 20 miles west and north to the Green River Crossing, located two and one-half miles north of the city of Green River where, in low water, an island divides the river. This position agrees well with Gunnison's distance of 20 miles from the point where he first reached the Spanish Trail.

Despite all of the traffic over the Spanish Trail, firsthand descriptions of the Green River Crossing are few indeed. The first we have was written by Orville Pratt, whom we have met before. In the service of the American government, Pratt, with an escort of sixteen men, reached the crossing on September 18, 1848. The river, swollen by recent heavy rain, was three hundred yards

ABOVE: *J. W. Powell River History Museum at Green River.*
S. K. MADSEN

RIGHT: *On his exploration of the Colorado River in 1871, John Wesley Powell named Gunnison Butte. Powell's party camped on the river opposite the butte and explored the river downstream to the Spanish Trail crossing.*
POWELL, EXPLORATION OF THE COLORADO RIVER OF THE WEST . . . (1875)

wide. The party swam the horses and rafted provisions and property across. Pratt thought of the Green as the "Rubicon of this California trip, & are, thanks to God, again wending our way westward." Pratt remarked that there are "fine fish in this stream." One of his men caught a six pound "mountain trout."

To popularize plans for a railroad across the central United States, E. F. Beale traveled over it en route to fill a government post in California. The Beale party arrived at the Green River Crossing on July 24, 1853, ahead of the Gunnison survey. Gwinn Harris Heap, press agent, artist, and diarist, described the crossing where the scenery was "grand and solemn." Anxious to get on to California to assume his post as superintendent of Indian affairs, Beale lost no time in crossing the river. A leather boat was built and some resident Utes, mounted and carrying rifles and "bows and quivers full of arrows with obsidian heads," watched these proceedings with considerable interest. When Beale left the boat to them, they promptly ripped it to pieces to salvage the leather for moccasin soles. Hurrying on over the Spanish Trail, the Beale expedition reached the Sevier River in four days, a distance, using Heap's figures, of 49 miles.

Another description of the Green River Crossing was written by Lt. E. G. Beckwith, second in command of the Gunnison railroad survey. On September 30, 1853, the Gunnison party camped on the Spanish Trail, on the eastern bank of the Green. The group was visited by some "Akanaquint or Green River" Indians encamped on the western bank, who quickly crossed over, by way of an island in the river, to trade. By their crossing, the Indians marked the historic ford on the

ABOVE LEFT: *Tamarisk surround the limited water of Trail Spring, the "Green River Spring" of the trail days.*

ABOVE: *Wild horses roam the land along the Spanish Trail in the San Rafael Swell.*

LEFT: *The natural tanks at Big Holes.*

Spanish Trail and, the next morning, the Gunnison party crossed the river without difficulty. The "red muddy" river was flowing swiftly, but the water did not rise above the axletrees of the wagons.

Two voyages of exploration down the Green and Colorado made by John Wesley Powell, 1869 and 1871-1872, brought the Green River Crossing further into national prominence. On the 1869 trip, the explorers stopped at the "old Spanish Crossing" July 13, where they enjoyed a noon rest under the "friendly shade of a cottonwood" before continuing on down the river. On the second voyage, Powell's party spent a week, August 26-September 1, 1871, at the Green River Crossing. Mindful of Gunnison's railroad survey, and of his death in 1853, Powell and his men named several landmarks for Gunnison: the great butte at the foot of Gray Canyon on the Green, the valley, and the Spanish Trail crossing. They observed the many signs of Indian life, past and present, along the river, and they described Gunnison's Crossing as "a great line of travel for the migratory bands of Utes that Arab-like dwell in these great valleys."[1]

History-minded travelers will want to visit the John Wesley Powell River History Museum on the east bank of the Green in Green River. The extensive galleries and exhibits portray John Wesley Powell's expeditions and furnish interpretation of Indian life, Spanish Trail caravans, fur trapping, government surveys, and river running. The museum, opened in 1990, contains a visitor center and gift shop.

[1] *See Crampton (1990) for a summary of the early explorers and the Green River Crossing.*

LEFT: *The extensive rock formations at Big Holes.* S. K. MADSEN

BELOW LEFT: *In 1880-83, the Denver & Rio Grande Western Railroad graded a line across the northern part of the San Rafael Swell. Tracks were never laid over the line which, for some distance, followed the Spanish Trail. Here, at a deep cut, the grade followed the trail near the base of Cedar Mountain in the background.*

BELOW: *The trail at Furniture Draw, San Rafael Swell.* S. K. MADSEN

SAN RAFAEL SWELL

From Green River, the Spanish Trail crosses the northern end of the San Rafael Swell, a huge, elongated upwarp in the earth's surface, eroded to form a labyrinth of canyons, dry washes, mesas, buttes, monoliths, and knobs. Across the Swell we found trail research challenging, but the accounts of John W. Gunnison, and of a Mormon party headed by Oliver B. Huntington, gave us important information.

Leaving Green River, Gunnison traveled to Trail Spring, known as Green River Spring in the trail days, and thence to Lost Spring Wash where he left the Spanish Trail, circling north around the difficult interior of the Swell, to carry on his railroad survey.

From Green River Spring, a mere stock watering pond today, the Spanish Trail emerges from the sands of Lost Spring Wash at Cement Crossing, on an unused grade of the Denver and Rio Grande Railroad. After engineering a 50-mile railroad bed that cut across the northern part of the Swell in 1882, the D&RG cancelled the project in favor of a direct route from Green River to Price, Utah. Sections of the abandoned grade closely parallel the Spanish Trail.

From Cement Crossing, the trail makes its way along Big Hole Wash toward the Big Holes, in Pack Saddle Gulch. Throughout this reach and beyond, we relied on the journal of Oliver B. Huntington, the official diarist of the 1855 Elk Mountain Mission, destined to found a settlement at Moab. The Mormons were the first to drive wagons across the San Rafael Swell. Huntington guides us to Big Holes, one of the most reliable places along the way. Here, water flowing over bedrock has created a series of natural tanks,

much used today by local stockmen.

Beyond Big Holes, the trail emerges into the open area passing between the broken rim of the San Rafael River drainage on the left and the thousand-foot-high cliffs of Cedar Mountain on the right.

It continues a west-northwest course to Little Holes, where water could be found in natural rock reservoirs, although it was nearly inaccessible to travelers. The difficulties of getting water here are described by Huntington who says: We "clambered down to an overhanging rock and drawed up water with lassos and then passed it from hand to hand until it reached the top. This was very dangerous work, occupied ten men. A little after dark all the stock had got a taste of water and very few all they wanted."[2] We investigated the Little Holes area and confirmed Huntington's description of it. Water

would have to have been lifted by ropes. We also found that, given a good water year, animals in some numbers could have been driven directly to ample pools of water at the head of the gulch.

From Little Holes, the trail advances westward, threading its way through Furniture Draw, then crosses Buckhorn Flat to reach the Black Hills and its northernmost point—approximately 39° 12' north latitude. From the Black Hills, the trail drops down to Huntington Creek in Castle Valley.

CASTLE VALLEY

Castle Valley, watered by streams falling from the high Wasatch Plateau immediately to the west, was settled in the 1870s by Mormon pioneers from central Utah who

---

[2] *Huntington (1855), 192.*

ABOVE: *The old Jorgensen Ranch near Castle Dale is located astride the Spanish Trail.*

ABOVE LEFT: *The castellated formations like these on Muddy Creek suggested the name Castle Valley.*

LEFT: *In 1853, Gunnison noted that the trail in Castle Valley was very distinct. Through the years, erosion has deepened the trail shown here on Walker Flat.*

followed Gunnison's wagon tracks—therefore, the Spanish Trail—across Emigrant, or Wasatch, Pass to their new homes. Settlements at Huntington, Castle Dale, Ferron, Emery, and others were established during the pioneer period. The Emery County Museum in Castle Dale features some collections relating to the valley's pioneer history.

Public land surveys followed settlement, and one must be especially grateful to government surveyor Augustus D. Ferron who very carefully laid down "Gunnison's Road" on his township plats, further identified in his notes as the "old Spanish Trail."[3]

You will recall that Gunnison left the Spanish Trail in the San Rafael Swell. He returned to it at Huntington Creek in Castle Valley. That he had little difficulty in following the Spanish Trail is evident from reading what he wrote about one section in Castle Valley: "The Spanish Trail though but seldom used of late years, is still very distinct where the soil washes but slightly. On some such spaces today we counted from fourteen to twenty parallel trails, of the ordinary size of Indian trails or horse paths, on a way of barely fifty feet in width."[4] Although most vestiges of the old trail in Castle Valley have disappeared, by using Ferron's township plats we were able to find short sections of the Spanish Trail in the Black Hills, on Cottonwood Creek, and on Ferron Creek.

[3] *Ferron (1873-1880).*
[4] *Beckwith (1855), 65.*

RIGHT: *Prehistoric pictograph on the wall of Ivie Creek Canyon is evidence of Indian usage of this passage centuries before it became the Spanish Trail.*
S. K. MADSEN

BELOW: *Interstate 70, (under construction, 1977), has entirely obliterated the Spanish Trail along Ivie Creek.*

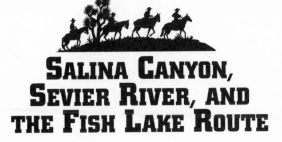

CHAPTER VI

SALINA CANYON, SEVIER RIVER, AND THE FISH LAKE ROUTE

From Castle Valley, the Spanish Trail, by way of Ivie Creek and Salina Canyon, crosses the elevated Wasatch Plateau and enters the eastern edge of the Great Basin. Beyond Salina Canyon, the trail turns up the Sevier River. The Fish Lake Route, a branch of the Spanish Trail between Ivie Creek and the Sevier River, crosses the Fish Lake Plateau and reaches elevations in excess of 9,000 feet, the highest points on the trail.

IVIE CREEK

Beyond Castle Valley, the Spanish Trail crosses Muddy Creek and its upper tributaries and, by way of Oak Spring Ranch, ascends one of them, Ivie Creek, to the summit of the Wasatch Plateau. The Spanish Trail along Ivie Creek is now covered by two parallel slabs of concrete, Interstate 70.

Prehistoric man came this way. Archaeologists tell us that the northern part of the Colorado Plateau was home to a people who followed the seasons, hunting animals and gathering wild plants. The Archaic, or Desert, lifeway began on the plateau more than 8,000 years ago (the pyramids had yet to be built in Egypt) and continued, intermittently, until about A.D. 500. At a site adjacent to Interstate 70, archaeologists have found a rock shelter which had been used by the Archaics for 5,000 years! From rock shelter to freeway! Historic

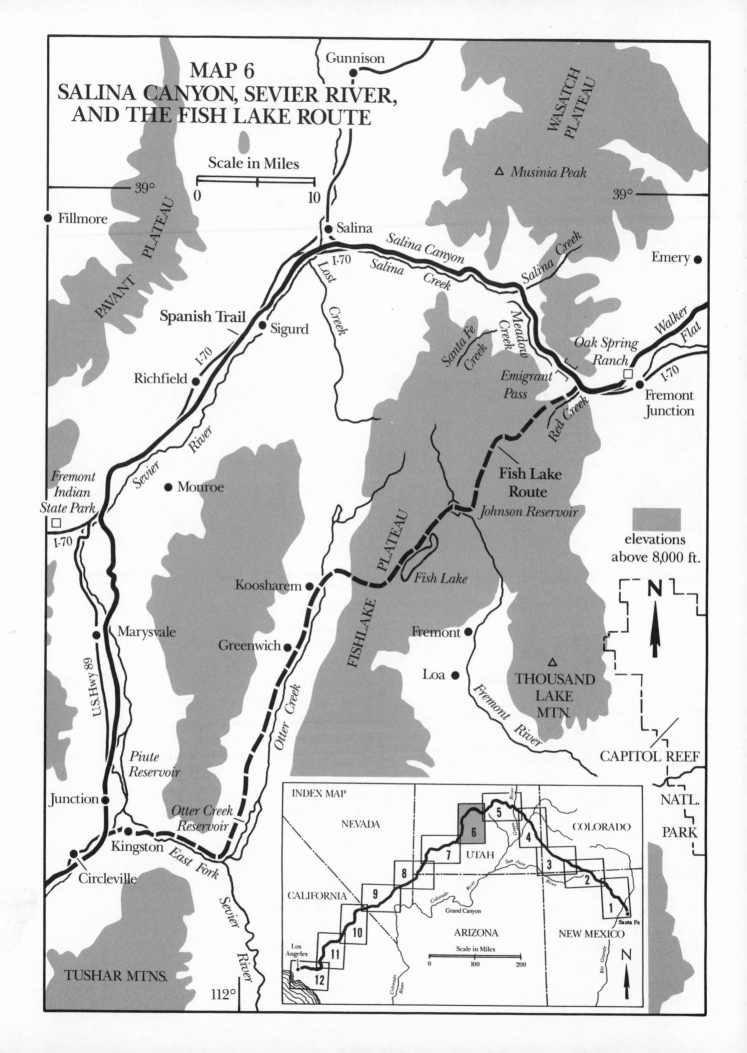

MAP 6
SALINA CANYON, SEVIER RIVER, AND THE FISH LAKE ROUTE

Scale in Miles

0   10

Gunnison

WASATCH PLATEAU

△ *Musinia Peak*

39°   39°

Fillmore

Salina

Emery

Salina Canyon

I-70

PAVANT PLATEAU

Salina Creek

Salina Creek

Lost Creek

Spanish Trail

Sigurd

Santa Fe Creek

Meadow Creek

Walker Flat

Oak Spring Ranch

I-70

Richfield

Emigrant Pass

Red Creek

Fremont Junction

Sevier River

Fish Lake Route

Fremont Indian State Park

Monroe

Johnson Reservoir

I-70

elevations above 8,000 ft.

N

Koosharem

FISHLAKE PLATEAU

Fish Lake

Fremont

Marysvale

Greenwich

Loa

THOUSAND LAKE MTN.

△

U.S. Hwy 89

Otter Creek

Fremont River

CAPITOL REEF

Piute Reservoir

NATL.

Junction

Otter Creek Reservoir

PARK

Kingston

East Fork

Circleville

Sevier River

TUSHAR MTNS.

112°

INDEX MAP

NEVADA

Green River

5

COLORADO

6

4

UTAH

7

San Juan River

3

8

2

Colorado River

CALIFORNIA

9

1

Grand Canyon

Santa Fe

10

ARIZONA

NEW MEXICO

Los Angeles

11

Colorado River

Rio Grande

12

Scale in Miles

0   100   200

N

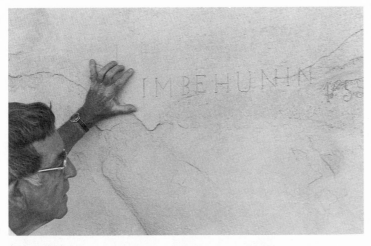

LEFT: *The name I. M. Behunin in Ivie Creek Canyon is a record of the passage of the Huntington Expedition in 1855.* S. K. MADSEN

BELOW LEFT: *Salina Canyon presented no serious obstacle for the Spanish Trail, but later users, including Gunnison, had to detour around rough places. Here a railroad company had to tunnel through the canyon wall at the Sawtooth Narrows.*

BELOW: *A local artist has painted a mural in downtown Salina depicting riders on the Spanish Trail.* S. K. MADSEN

human passageway from the Colorado Plateau to the Great Basin.[1] A dramatic pictograph on the canyon wall at one point was probably painted by some prehistoric artist long before Columbus discovered America. Gunnison saw the painting in 1853; it was fully described by the Huntington expedition in 1855.[2]

Going up Ivie Creek (to which he gave the Indian name Akanaquint), Gunnison came to a fork in the trail at the mouth of Red Creek. The "southern branch" of the Spanish Trail split off here. Going by way of Fish Lake and the East Fork of the Sevier River, this was the shortest route, but it reached elevations in excess of 9,000 feet, and it probably saw less use than the longer "northern branch," which crossed Emigrant, or Wasatch, Pass at an elevation of approximately 7,800 feet. Both tracks join again at the confluence of the

Sevier River and its east fork (see Fish Lake Route). At the pass, the Spanish Trail crosses from the Colorado River drainage to the Great Basin.

The vast Great Basin in the interior of western North America, with no outlet to the sea, was identified and named by John C. Frémont during the course of his second expedition, 1843-1844. His conclusion as to its existence was made while he was riding the Spanish Trail between Cajon Pass and the Little Salt Lake.

SALINA CANYON

From Emigrant Pass, the Spanish Trail follows Salina Canyon to the Sevier River, a natural route that posed few difficulties for

---

[1] *Schroedl (1979), 347-349.*
[2] *Crampton (1990); Beckwith (1855), 66; and Huntington (1855), 190-191.*

LEFT: *Petroglyphs near museum building, Fremont Indian State Park.*

BELOW: *A pastoral scene in the Sevier River Valley.*

pack trains. Or for highways. The Spanish Trail throughout Salina Canyon now lies beneath the pavement of Interstate 70.

In 1853, Gunnison, with his wagon train, left the Spanish Trail to make a lengthy detour (used by later wagon traffic) around the rocky Sawtooth Narrows, about 15 miles above the mouth of Salina Canyon. Once out of the mountains at the present city of Salina, Gunnison turned north down the Sevier River. Nine days later, on October 26, 1853, he and several members of his party were killed by Paiute Indians.

SEVIER RIVER VALLEY

Leaving the rough country behind, westbound travelers found easy going for about 30 miles as they traveled south up the valley of the Sevier River (the Rio Severo of the trail days). Here, in the agricultural heartland of central Utah, there was plenty of water and grass, if little wood, along the meandering stream. Orville Pratt was mightily impressed with the valley's ambience in late September 1848, when he wrote: "it was truly the loveliest spot, all things considered, my eyes have ever looked upon."[3] Gwinn Harris Heap, of the Beale Survey, passing through the valley in late July 1853, wrote that it "surpassed in beauty and fertility anything we have yet seen."[4] We agree with Heap that the Spanish Trail probably stayed to the west of the Sevier River, paralleling the modern highway. Passing through Richfield and Elsinore, the trail continues on to a point near the mouth of Clear Creek coming in from the west.

The Sevier River Valley was certainly

---

[3] *Pratt (1954), 352.*

[4] *Heap (1957), 219.*

64

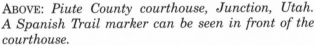

ABOVE: *Piute County courthouse, Junction, Utah. A Spanish Trail marker can be seen in front of the courthouse.*

ABOVE RIGHT: *The abundant waters and grass of the Sevier River were the best on the Spanish Trail.* S. K. MADSEN

RIGHT: *An engraving from the work by Brewerton, who popularized the Fish Lake Route in his travels with Kit Carson in 1848.* STALLO VINTON, ED., OVERLAND WITH KIT CARSON . . . BY GEORGE BREWERTON (1930)

home to prehistoric peoples, notably the Fremont Indians who lived in the region beginning about the first century A.D. We found that the new Fremont Indian State Park, a few miles from the mouth of Clear Creek on Interstate 70, is a splendid place to study the Fremont Culture. Here, a perfectly designed museum displays the full range of this prehistoric culture. The museum itself is located in the center of a very extensive Fremont settlement. Visitors may walk about through the site and view petroglyphs and other remains of this distinctive culture.[5]

After visiting the park, we returned to the Spanish Trail where it left the Sevier to detour to the east around the narrow, rocky Marysvale Canyon. Driving over dirt roads, we followed the trail up over a divide a thousand feet above the river, where we found the way open, with few obstacles to passage. The

trail reaches the river again in the vicinity of Marysvale. It continues up the Sevier about 18 miles to its confluence with the East Fork near the town of Junction, where the Fish Lake route joins the main Spanish Trail.

FISH LAKE ROUTE

The Fish Lake route of the Spanish Trail, between Ivie Creek and Junction on the Sevier River, was an alternate route popularized by George D. Brewerton and Kit Carson. This route leaves the main trail at Red Creek, and quickly ascends to a high ridge, and crosses the divide to the basin of Fish Lake on the headwaters of the Fremont River. The trail passes through Johnson Valley Reservoir and continues on along the west shore of Fish Lake, elevation 8,843 feet.

---

[5] Kohler (1989).

RIGHT: *A section of the Spanish Trail on upper Otter Creek. The town of Koosharem appears in the distance.*

BELOW: *Old schoolhouse at Greenwich on the Spanish Trail in Otter Creek Valley.*

Brewerton called it Trout Lake. While camped here with his party, he bought a fine trout from some visiting Indians for a "couple charges of powder." Then some of the men found a tributary stream swarming with fish. To Brewerton's party, suffering from hunger, this "was *more* than good news." That evening all hands enjoyed a feast of simple fish chowder.[6]

From Fish Lake, the Spanish Trail crosses from the Colorado Plateau to the Great Basin, dropping down into Grass Valley, drained by Otter Creek. The trail follows down Otter Creek to its junction with the East Fork of the Sevier River at the Otter Creek Reservoir. Here, it turns west along the East Fork to join the main trail near Junction.

Although the trail may be easily seen for the first few miles beyond Ivie Creek, the terrain is very steep and rocky, and access is difficult. Today's travelers following the trail should plan to do some hiking here.

_____

[6] *Vinton, ed. (1930), 109-111.*

ABOVE: *Rail fence on the high northern reaches of the Markagunt Plateau.*

RIGHT: *The Butch Cassidy home near Circleville.*

CHAPTER VII

CIRCLEVILLE TO MOUNTAIN MEADOWS

The Spanish Trail from Junction to Circleville roughly follows present U.S. 89. Beyond Circleville in Sevier River Valley, it crosses the high Markagunt Plateau to reach an open region which the Mormons, in the 1850s, found suitable for settlement. At this point, we are helped along in our study of the Spanish Trail by the diary and map of John C. Frémont, who traveled this far on the trail from California in 1844. At Mountain Meadows, the trail leaves the Great Basin to return to the watershed of the Colorado River.

CIRCLEVILLE

During the Spanish Trail days, the Sevier above the East Fork was known as Rio San Pascual. We followed the trail for about 23 miles through Circle Valley and Circleville Canyon, where there is no obstacle to passage. Throughout this distance, today's traveler will be impressed by the meadows with cattle grazing, and by the high mountain peaks rising on either side. In this pastoral setting, Circleville enjoys the quiet serenity that can be felt while driving through much of the Sevier River Valley.

One of the Spanish Trail's claims to fame is the fact that Robert LeRoy Parker, alias Butch Cassidy, was raised in a log cabin near Circleville!

BEAR VALLEY

Not far from the head of Circleville

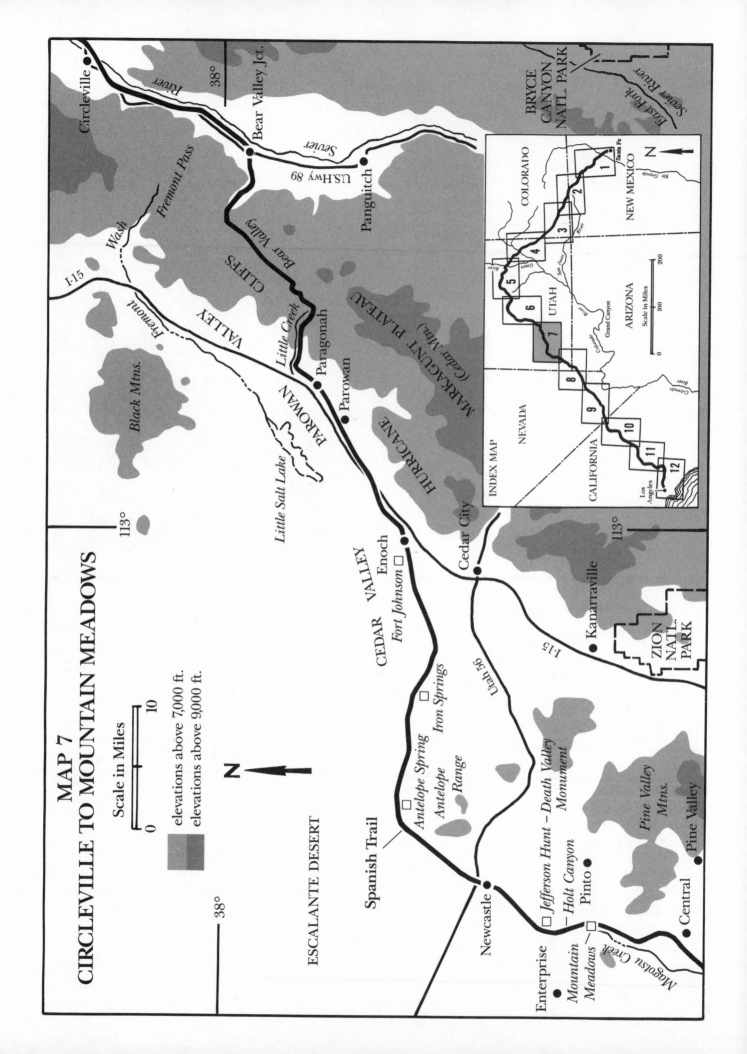

MAP 7
CIRCLEVILLE TO MOUNTAIN MEADOWS

Scale in Miles

0   10

N

elevations above 7,000 ft.
elevations above 9,000 ft.

Circleville

Bear Valley Jct.

38°

River

Fremont Pass

Sevier

Wash

U.S.Hwy 89

Panguitch

Fremont

I-15

CLIFFS

Little Creek

Bear Valley

Paragonah

Parowan

Black Mtns.

VALLEY

PAROWAN

Little Salt Lake

HURRICANE

MARKAGUNT PLATEAU
(Cedar Mtns.)

113°

38°

113°

CEDAR VALLEY

Enoch

Fort Johnson

Cedar City

Kanarraville

ZION NATL. PARK

I-15

Utah 56

ESCALANTE DESERT

Spanish Trail

Iron Springs

Antelope Spring

Antelope Range

Jefferson Hunt – Death Valley Monument

Holt Canyon

Pinto

Newcastle

Pine Valley Mtns.

Pine Valley

Central

Enterprise

Mountain Meadows

Magotsu Creek

INDEX MAP

N

Santa Fe

COLORADO

NEW MEXICO

Rio Grande

1

2

3

4

5

6

7

8

9

10

11

12

UTAH

Green River

San Juan River

Colorado River

ARIZONA

Grand Canyon

Colorado River

NEVADA

CALIFORNIA

Los Angeles

Scale in Miles

0   100   200

BRYCE CANYON NATL. PARK

East Fork Sevier River

Sevier River

LEFT: *The bed of Little Salt Lake, dry in recent times, was a permanent body of water during Mexican caravan days.* S. K. MADSEN

BELOW: *Names on the rocks in Fremont Pass, a route across the Markagunt north of the Spanish Trail.*

Canyon, the trail reaches Bear Valley Junction where it leaves the Sevier, turning abruptly to the west. The way thence is across the northern end of the Markagunt Plateau by a natural route, following up Bear Creek through Lower and Upper Bear Valley. Crossing a divide, the trail heads down Little Creek, a rough and rocky route which passes through the upthrust Hurricane Cliffs before dramatically breaking out into the open near the town of Paragonah in Parowan Valley.

Orville Pratt in 1848 describes the trail down Little Creek as "a very hilly & rocky country—Sometimes up the steepest of hills, then down places which it would seem almost impossible to descend, again in deep and precipitous canions."[1]

Our guides through much of the Sevier River Valley, and Bear Valley, are Orville Pratt and the map prepared by Gwinn Harris Heap in his account of the Beale exploration.

Some writers have identified Frémont's crossing of the Markagunt Plateau with the Spanish Trail. However, on his fifth expedition, during mid-winter 1853-54, Frémont crossed the Markagunt by way of Fremont Pass and Fremont Canyon, about 14 miles north of the Spanish Trail in Upper Bear Valley. Suffering from exposure and hunger, and in desperate straits, the Frémont party was nursed back to health by the Mormons in the new settlement of Parowan.[2] The

---

[1] Pratt (1954), 353.

[2] Jackson and Spence, eds. (1970). The best edition of Frémont's writings has been prepared by Donald Jackson and Mary Lee Spence, a set of four volumes and map portfolio. Volume one contains Frémont's account of the second expedition (1843-44). We have frequently cited the 1843-44 Frémont expedition, since Frémont gives an on-the-spot description of the Spanish Trail from a point near Cajon Pass to Little Salt Lake. Volume three covers the fifth expedition.

ABOVE: *Cabin on the Spanish Trail dating back to the beginnings of settlement at Elkhorn Springs (Fort Johnson).*

ABOVE RIGHT: *Copy of the marker prepared by William R. Palmer who organized the Spanish Trail Association.* COPY OF ORIGINAL IN UTAH STATE HISTORICAL SOCIETY

RIGHT: *In some places in Cedar Valley the Spanish Trail is clearly visible.*

Fremont Pass route had been used by the Parley P. Pratt exploring expedition through southern Utah in 1849.

PAROWAN VALLEY

Orville Pratt describes the view of Parowan Valley and Little Salt Lake as his expedition reached Paragonah on October 1, l848:

> [There] suddenly broke upon us one of the finest and most extensive valleys I have seen in the whole western country! In the center of it was a fine lake full of fish, with gravelly banks, and into which run 4 fine mountain streams from the south & about 6 mi. apart. This valley is about 20 m. long & 10 broad. Camped on one of these creeks.

Orville Pratt's description of the Parowan Valley is fair enough, but his fish story is quite an exaggeration.

On his second expedition in 1844, Frémont traveled along the west bank of Little Salt Lake, which he identified on his map as a Salt Lake, and wrote of it as follows: "This little lake, which well merits its characteristic name, lies immediately at the base of the Wah-satch Range, and nearly opposite a gap in that chain of mountains through which the Spanish trail passes...." Of course, the "gap" in Frémont's account is the mouth of Little Creek Canyon.

Travelers on the Spanish Trail had an easy time of it as they crossed the open Parowan Valley, where the pioneer Mormon towns of Paragonah and Parowan were founded in the early 1850s. Beyond Parowan a short distance, Pratt reached "St. Jose Spring" (Frémont's "Saint Joseph Spring"), and described it as "one of the finest fountains and streams of water on the entire

RIGHT: *The Spanish Trail has often been confused with the trail opened by the Spanish friars, Domínguez and Escalante in 1776. Bound for California, the friars left Santa Fe and traveled through western Colorado and northern and central Utah. When their party reached Cedar Valley, they decided to turn back to Santa Fe. The only place where the Spanish Trail followed the Domínguez-Escalante track was in New Mexico and Colorado. In Cedar Valley, the Spanish Trail crossed the Domínguez-Escalante track at right angles, since the party was headed south on its return to New Mexico. The marker shown here in Cedar Valley (Highway 56) is one of the many placed as a bicentennial project of New Mexico, Colorado, Utah, and Arizona.*

BOTTOM RIGHT: *S. Alva Matheson of Cedar City guides researchers over the trail through Cedar Valley to Newcastle. Matheson is pictured here at Antelope Spring.*

route."[3] This watering place on the Spanish Trail is identical with the once-bountiful springs bursting from the ground near the town of Enoch, first known as Elkhorn Springs.

From Parowan Valley to the Utah-Arizona boundary and beyond, there is much more documentation to assist us in locating the Spanish Trail. Coming from California on his second expedition in 1844, John C. Frémont followed the Spanish Trail to Parowan Valley where he left it. His diary and map of the route provided guidance for the Mormons who, shortly after founding their wilderness kingdom on the shores of the Great Salt Lake in 1847, turned the old trail into a passable wagon road all the way to Los Angeles. Thus, after 1848, this section of the trail came to be known as the Mormon, or Salt Lake, Trail, or the California Road. The journals of Frémont,

early Mormon travelers, and others who knew they were traveling on the Spanish Trail, make up an impressive body of primary documents. With these sources at hand, we can, with considerable confidence, follow the Spanish Trail throughout the remainder of its course.

CEDAR CITY

Cedar City, the home of Southern Utah University, a few miles from the Spanish Trail, is a significant place for research on the old trail. Some years ago, the late William R. Palmer of Cedar City organized the Spanish Trail Association to mark the historic trail. Many of the markers placed by the association may still be seen on public buildings and other places in and near cities and towns

[3] *Pratt (1954), 353.*

RIGHT: *On the trail near Antelope Spring.* S. K. MADSEN

BELOW: *Public interest in the Spanish Trail is manifest in this sign at Newcastle.*

along the way in Utah. Palmer assembled a large collection of materials on the Spanish Trail, and these may be consulted in the Palmer Western History Collection in Special Collections in the library of Southern Utah University.

Cedar City is the seat of Iron County, so-called because the Mormon pioneers, having discovered iron ore to the west at Iron Springs, built here the first iron smelter west of the Mississippi River. Visitors to Cedar City should stop in at the Iron Mission State Historical Monument featuring the history of southern Utah and early transportation. The museum numbers over 100 horse-drawn vehicles in its collections.

TO THE DEATH VALLEY CUTOFF

Staying in open country for approximately 45 miles, the trail from Enoch crosses Cedar Valley and the southern edge of the Escalante Desert to the mouth of Holt Canyon. Throughout this entire distance, S. Alva Matheson of Cedar City served as our guide. He pointed out important places along the Spanish Trail, including the key watering holes at Iron Springs, Antelope Spring, and Pinto Creek at Newcastle. Addison Pratt on November 2, 1849, describes Antelope Spring as follows: It was "on the mountain side. The spring oozes out of the ground and makes a large stream which, after running a few rods, sinks back into the ground."[4] The spring is used as a water source by cattlemen today.

About six miles from Newcastle, adjacent to the Spanish Trail, the Jefferson Hunt-Death Valley monument marks the place

---

[4] *Hafen and Hafen, eds.,* Journals of Forty-Niners *(1954a), 78.*

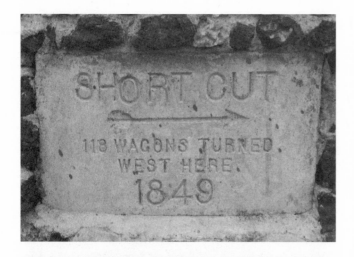

ABOVE: *Jefferson Hunt-Death Valley Monument.*

ABOVE LEFT: *The Jefferson Hunt Monument also indicates the number of wagons which headed west on the cutoff to Death Valley. The monument was placed on public land not far from the Spanish Trail.*

LEFT: *Storm clouds over Mountain Meadows.*

where a large body of California-bound Forty-niners decided to take a short cut to the gold fields and left the established Spanish Trail at this point. It was they who found themselves in Death Valley, and whose misfortunes in escaping it gave the valley its name. See Hafen and Hafen, eds., *Journals of Forty-Niners*, for details concerning the departure from the wagon train led by Jefferson Hunt. About a mile west of the Jefferson Hunt monument, the Spanish Trail turns up Holt Canyon to Mountain Meadows.

MOUNTAIN MEADOWS

Riding southward up Holt Canyon, also known as Meadow Canyon, for six miles, the early travelers came to Mountain Meadows, a cool (elevation about 5,900 feet), open area of abundant grass and water, four or five miles long, on the divide between the Great Basin and the Colorado River drainage. Known in the trail days as the "Vegas de Santa Clara," this was a favorite resting and regrouping place, especially for those eastbound parties pulling up out of the desert country below.

John C. Frémont, whose journal guides us from the Parowan Valley to a point near Cajon Pass in California, describes "las Vegas de Santa Clara" on May 12, 1844: "We found here an extensive mountain meadow, rich in bunch grass, and fresh with numerous springs of clear water, all refreshing and delightful to look upon."

Orville Pratt described Mountain Meadows on October 5, 1848: "The animals are doing finely on the excellent grass they get here. There is fine & tender grass enough growing on this Vegas to fatten a thousand head of horses or cattle."

George D. Brewerton, who accompanied

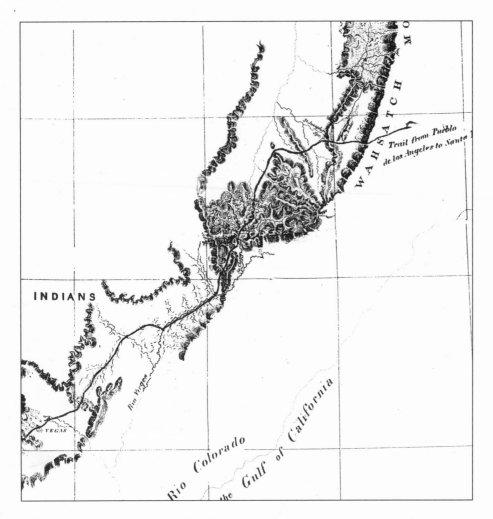

Section of J. C. Frémont's Map of an Exploring Expedition . . . to Oregon and North California in 1843-1844, published in 1845. The map, showing much white space, depicts only the region actually explored by Frémont. We can trace the Spanish Trail all the way from Salt Lake (Little Salt Lake) to St. Joseph's Spring (Elkhorn Springs at Enoch), to the Vegas de Santa Clara (Mountain Meadows), to Santa Clara [River], to Rio Virgen (Virgin River), to [Las] Vegas. Frémont was following the Spanish Trail, and thus we have an accurate map of the route between the places indicated.
MAP, FRÉMONT (1845)
(TRAIL ENHANCED)

Kit Carson in 1848 over the Spanish Trail, gives us this view of Mountain Meadows: "The noise of running water, the large grassy meadows, from which the spot takes its name, and the green hills which circle it round—all tend to captivate the eye and please the senses of the way-worn *voyageur*."[5]

The history of the place will always be associated with the infamous Mountain Meadows Massacre, where in 1857, for a complex of reasons, some fanatic Mormons and Indians massacred a train of emigrants coming from Missouri and Arkansas. A new monument, dedicated September 15, 1990, on Magotsu Creek, one of the heads of the Santa Clara River, marks the spot. See Juanita Brooks, *The Mountain Meadows Massacre* for a balanced treatment of the tragedy.

At the monument marking the massacre site, one may note that the bed of Magotsu Creek has deeply eroded. This is a good example of the erosion that takes place when trails are developed in soft soil in desert country. Water flowing downhill quickly cuts an arroyo following the trail pattern, and this continues cutting, where adjacent vegetation may have been removed by grazing animals. During our field investigations, we found numbers of "trail-shaped" arroyos on the Spanish Trail.[6]

[5] *Jackson and Spence, eds. (1970), I, 692; Pratt (1954), 354; and Vinton, ed. (1930), 99.*
[6] *Ivins (1924); and Cottam (1961).*

ABOVE: *Ranch along the Santa Clara River. Pine Valley Mountain appears in the distance.*

LEFT: *The owners of this mercantile at Veyo on the Santa Clara River show an awareness of their historical heritage.*

CHAPTER VIII

THE VIRGIN RIVER: UTAH, ARIZONA, NEVADA

From Mountain Meadows, the Spanish Trail enters the basin of the Virgin River. The trail descends the Santa Clara River, a Virgin River tributary, and crosses the Beaver Dam Mountains to reach the main stream near Beaver Dam in Arizona. It descends along the Virgin River, then leaves the river to cross Mormon Mesa in Nevada. This section of the trail, with its Indian populations and typical desert flora, was described by John C. Frémont who passed over it on his second expedition in 1844.

SANTA CLARA RIVER

Leaving Mountain Meadows, the Spanish Trail parallels the modern highway to Central, where it turns down the tributaries of Magotsu Creek and Moody Wash to the main Santa Clara River (named on Frémont's map of his second expedition). We followed the trail along these branches and the main stream for about 25 miles. Today, the village of Gunlock on the Santa Clara, founded in 1857, is a reminder of early Mormon settlement in southwestern Utah. Downstream, the Shivwits Indian Reservation reminds us that, for many centuries, this was Paiute territory.

The Spanish Trail, running from the Sevier River Valley in Utah, through Las Vegas in Nevada, to the Mojave Desert in California, passed through homelands of the Southern Paiute Indians, linguistic relatives of the Utes. Living in a formidable desert

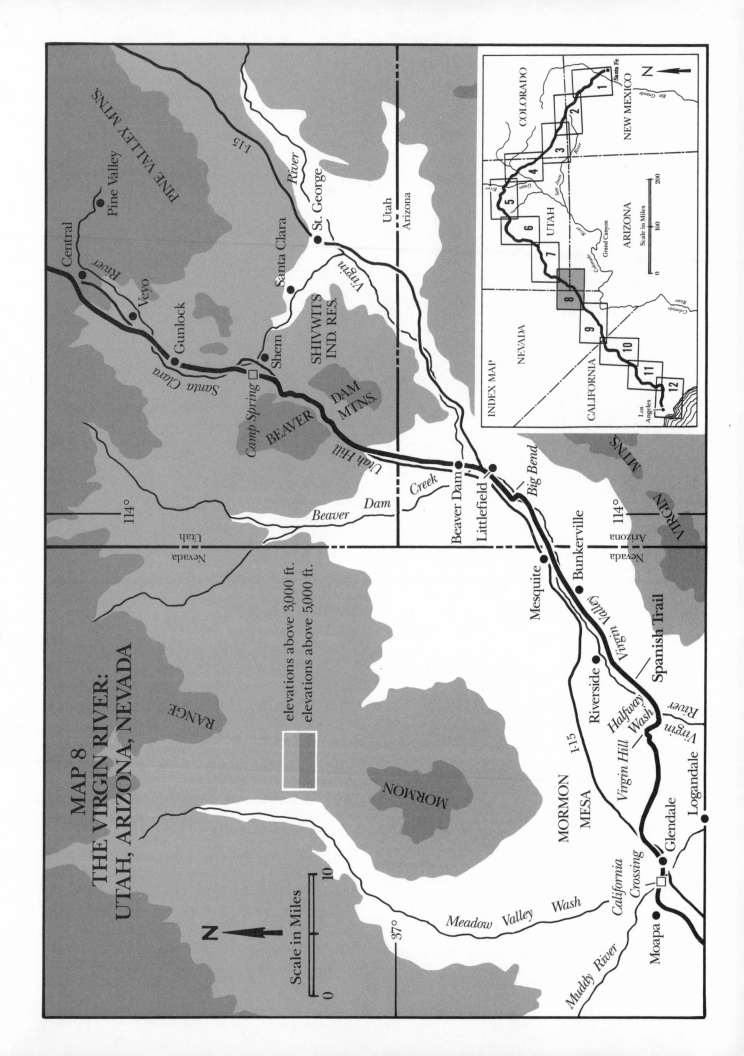

MAP 8
THE VIRGIN RIVER:
UTAH, ARIZONA, NEVADA

elevations above 3,000 ft.
elevations above 5,000 ft.

Scale in Miles

N

0
10

PINE VALLEY MTNS.

Pine Valley

Central

Veyo

River

Gunlock

Santa Clara

Santa Clara

Shem

Camp Spring

BEAVER

DAM
MTNS.

Utah Hill

SHIVWITS
IND. RES.

St. George

River

Virgin

I-15

Utah
Arizona

Beaver

Dam

Creek

Beaver Dam

Littlefield

Big Bend

Bunkerville

Mesquite

VIRGIN
MTNS.

Nevada
Arizona

114°

Virgin Valley

Spanish Trail

Riverside

Halfway Wash

Virgin Hill Wash

Virgin River

MORMON
MESA

I-15

MORMON
RANGE

114°

Utah
Nevada

37°

Meadow

Valley

Wash

California Crossing

Glendale

Logandale

Muddy River

Moapa

INDEX MAP

COLORADO

NEW MEXICO

Santa Fe

1

2

3

4

5

6

7

8

9

10

11

12

UTAH

Green River

San Juan

Rio Grande

ARIZONA

Grand Canyon

Colorado River

NEVADA

CALIFORNIA

Los Angeles

N

Scale in Miles

200

100

0

Jacob Hamblin and John Wesley Powell (seated together, right center) hold a conference with Paiute Indians, ca. 1872. UTAH STATE HISTORICAL SOCIETY

Paiute man, photographed about 1873.
MUSEUM OF THE AMERICAN INDIAN, NEW YORK CITY

environment, the Paiutes made skillful use of the limited natural resources. They lived in small encampments and moved about hunting and gathering. Along the Santa Clara, Virgin, and Muddy rivers, they developed small farms.

The Southern Paiutes were little affected by the coming of the white man until the opening of the Spanish Trail. Thereafter, the passing caravans left the desert trampled and denuded. The Indians were victimized by slave catchers, raiders, and traders who took captive women and children for sale as domestics to the settlements in California and New Mexico. The Paiutes were not horse breeders and could not defend themselves, at least during the early years of the trail, when mounted Utes, notably the notorious Walker (Wakara and other spellings), plundered them regularly. Slave-catching was a sideline business, practiced by numbers of New Mexican traders. During the later trail years, the Paiutes fought back, as Frémont observed in 1844, but fear of the slavers drove many of the Indians away from the trail area.[1]

Riding along the Santa Clara River in 1853, Gwinn Harris Heap observed that the Indians were fearful that his party might be slavers. He reported that a woman hid her child in a wicker basket, and when one of the party looked into the basket, he saw "a little naked fellow, his teeth chattering with fear."[2]

---

[1] *D'Azevedo, ed. (1986) Volume 11: Great Basin contains recent research on the Southern Paiute Indians, including material on slave catching and trading by travelers on the Spanish Trail. The Ute chief, Walker, has received considerable scholarly attention. His role in Spanish Trail history is briefly examined in Crampton, ed. (1971).*
[2] *Heap (1957), 235.*

ALL PHOTOS ABOVE: *Pioneer register at Camp Spring. J. E. Ide was a member of the military expedition headed by George F. Price in 1864.*

In 1854, Jacob Hamblin and other Mormons established a mission among the Paiutes downstream at Santa Clara, a short distance from the Spanish Trail. The success of the Indian mission at Santa Clara preceded the rapid settlement of the region by Mormons, who founded St. George in 1861, in the heart of what became Utah's "Dixie." Within a few years, John Wesley Powell and G. W. Ingalls undertook a thorough study of the Paiute Indians, living along the Spanish Trail and elsewhere, for the federal government.[3]

CAMP SPRING

At a point where the Santa Clara River makes a bend to join with the Virgin River, the Spanish Trail caravans left the river and started the climb over the Beaver Dam Mountains. Camp Spring, less than two miles

from the river, doesn't figure much in trail literature, but inscriptions on the rocks nearby have puzzled recent visitors. Doing some detective work, we consulted government documents and discovered the history behind some of the inscriptions.

It seems that in 1864, Colonel Patrick Edward Connor, commander at Camp Douglas in Salt Lake City, sent a military expedition under Captain George F. Price, Company M, Second Cavalry, USA, to open a military route to the head of navigation on the Colorado River. The command traveled in wagons through Mountain Meadows, where the soldiers erected a rock monument in memory of victims of the Mountain Meadows massacre. A few days later, after a long haul down the Santa Clara, the command made a

---

[3] *Powell and Ingalls (1874).*

RIGHT: *On Utah Hill, the Spanish Trail threads its way through a forest of giant Joshuas.*

BELOW: *An arroyo heading at lower right corner of photograph outlines the Spanish Trail for several miles beyond Camp Spring.*

rest stop at Camp Spring, where some of the men took time to add their names and military affiliations to a pioneer register on nearby rocks.

With ailing animals, Price followed the Spanish Trail to Las Vegas, turned south and, after many hardships, reached Fort Mohave on the Colorado River. At that point, Captain Price reported that the detachment was "completely worn out and exhausted, half the men barefooted, horses scarcely able to walk." Nevertheless, Price thought that his wagon-borne expedition was a success and recommended that further investigations be undertaken.[4]

The Spanish Trail was a pack trail. In many places it was not easily converted to a wagon road. In this book, we are citing a number of those who tried to do so, since their adventures tell us much about the old trail.

UTAH HILL

From Camp Spring, we determined that the Spanish Trail follows a course practically identical with old U.S. Highway 91. Crossing a pass in the Beaver Dam Mountains at an elevation of about 4,800 feet, it starts down the long "Utah Hill," best known in the early days of the automobile as the place where radiators always boiled over on the upgrade. Near the summit, at Castle Cliff, a service station was built in the 1920s to serve drivers of ailing automobiles. The remains of this place is now called the "Old Spanish Trail Ranch" by a new owner.

On Utah Hill, west-bound riders on the Spanish Trail got their first view of the spectacular giant Joshua tree *(Yucca brevifolia)*, a plant marking the eastern limits of the

[4] *McCarthy (1975), 139-143; and Price (1897), 355-360.*

ABOVE: *Castle Cliff Rest, a garden stop at the landmark Castle Cliff, serviced travelers on old Highway 91. The buildings have been removed or have fallen into disrepair. The location is now known as the Old Spanish Trail Ranch.* G. M. AND C. W. SMITH

LEFT: *Beaver Dam Wash near its mouth in Arizona.*

Mojave Desert. The name was given by a Mormon party traveling the Spanish Trail to San Bernardino in 1851. The story is told that on Utah Hill, when clouds covered the burning sun, the leader of the company, Elisha Hunt, cried out: "Look brethren! The sky is no longer like brazen brass! God has sent the clouds. It is as if the sun stood still—as Joshua commanded. These green trees are lifting their arms to heaven in supplication. We shall call them Joshua Trees. . . ."[5]

On Utah Hill, the Spanish Trail crosses the Utah-Arizona boundary at 729.246 miles from Santa Fe.

BEAVER DAM

At the bottom of Utah Hill, just below the old resort community of Beaver Dam, Arizona, the Spanish Trail crosses the Beaver Dam Wash near its mouth, at an elevation of 1,837 feet above sea level, the lowest point thus far on the trail. Owing to this elevation, the lower section of the wash is an oasis lying in a transition zone between the Colorado Plateau, the Great Basin, and the Mojave Desert. Numerous plants and animals, characteristic of these three geographical provinces, exist here in a rare desert setting. Beavers have been damming the stream at the Spanish Trail crossing for many years.

The Lytle Ranch, some miles upstream from the Spanish Trail, has been preserved as a permanent laboratory for the study of this ecosytem.

VIRGIN RIVER

Rio Virgen Frémont called it in 1844, and laid it down on his great map of the second

---

[5] *Murbarger (1947), 6.*

The Virgin River below Mesquite, Nevada. Riders on the Spanish Trail found it necessary to cross and recross the stream many times.

expedition. Heading up on the high Markagunt Plateau, the Virgin flows through the great gorge of Zion National Park. Then, it breaks out in the open for some miles as it flows through Utah's Dixie, before entering another gorge—the Virgin Narrows.

Below the Narrows, at the mouth of Beaver Dam Wash, the Spanish Trail reaches the Virgin river. It stays high on the right bank for several miles, and then descends to the river bed over a gravel terrace, just above the Big Bend. Here again we noticed rust marks on the cobblestones like those we had seen on the steep slope on the west side of the Animas River. For approximately 18 miles beyond the Big Bend, passing Mesquite and Bunkerville in Nevada, the trail follows the river, crossing and recrossing the stream ten times or more.

Frémont traveled up the Virgin River for several days in May of 1844. He described the Virgin as "the most dreary river I have ever seen—a deep rapid stream, almost a torrent, passing swiftly by, and roaring against obstructions." Some spring runoff! Frémont also observed that the Indians were everywhere about, ready to drive off any tired animals left behind.[6]

VIRGIN HILL

At Halfway Wash, the Spanish Trail left the Virgin River. At this point, the caravans had to pull through two miles of sand to the foot of Mormon Mesa. To reach the top of the mesa, they had to go up Virgin Hill, the steepest place on the entire trail. Here the trail climbs a grade of over 13 percent.

Frémont passed here in May of 1844, but

[6] *Jackson and Spence, eds. (1970), I, 689.*

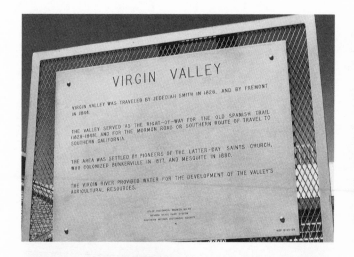

ABOVE: *Indian mortars on the rocks above the Virgin River as it flows past Littlefield, Arizona.*

ABOVE LEFT: *State historical marker in Mesquite, Nevada.*

LEFT: *Aerial view of the Spanish Trail climbing Virgin Hill on Mormon Mesa.*

he says nothing of the descent from Mormon Mesa to the Virgin River. Horsemen going down or up this hill would not have had great difficulty in the passage, but later travelers in wagons found the hill to be extremely difficult. For instance: David W. Cheesman in 1850 reported "leaving the Virgin and going up an arroyo" to Virgin Hill. To ascend the lower bench of the hill, he found it necessary to triple the oxen teams. To reach the second bench, or top of the hill, Cheesman drove the animals to the rim, then drew the wagons up by chaining them to the yoked oxen.[7]

Lieutenant Sylvester Mowry in 1855 says: The hill "is one of the worst I ever saw. Ten mules were used on each of the wagons, and my small train was two and a half hours getting on to the plateau."[8]

In his telegraphic style, Captain Price in 1864 reports: "Leaving the Rio Virgin for Muddy, had to rise a large hill, a mile long. At that point was compelled to pack outfit on horses; then place all mules to wagons, and sixty men with ropes in addition to get them on top of the hill."[9] Leaving the Virgin River near the mouth of Halfway Wash, a later, very steep, wagon road was opened to the top of the mesa. Captain Price may have been describing this later road.

Probably few of the riders cresting Virgin Hill on the Spanish Trail took any time to enjoy the view of the Virgin River Valley and the Virgin Mountains rising to over 8,000 feet on the eastern horizon. Those following the Spanish Trail today will see numbers of red barrel cactus (ferocactus) on the rim of the mesa near the top of the trail. To alleviate

[7] *Foy, ed. (1930), 293.*
[8] *Bailey, ed. (1965), 338.*
[9] *Price (1897), 355.*

LEFT: *Upper section of Virgin Hill at the rim of Mormon Mesa.*

BELOW LEFT: *Lower section of Spanish Trail on Virgin Hill.*

BELOW: *Senior author on the top of Virgin Hill on Mormon Mesa, on a hot day in August.* S. K. MADSEN

thirst, Frémont mentions that "we ate occasionally the *bisnada* [barrel cactus]."[10] Once on top of the mesa, caravans on the Spanish Trail crossed an open, nearly flat, desert country for about 11 miles before dropping down rapidly to the Muddy River near Glendale, Nevada.

---

[10] *Jackson and Spence, eds. (1970), I, 686.*

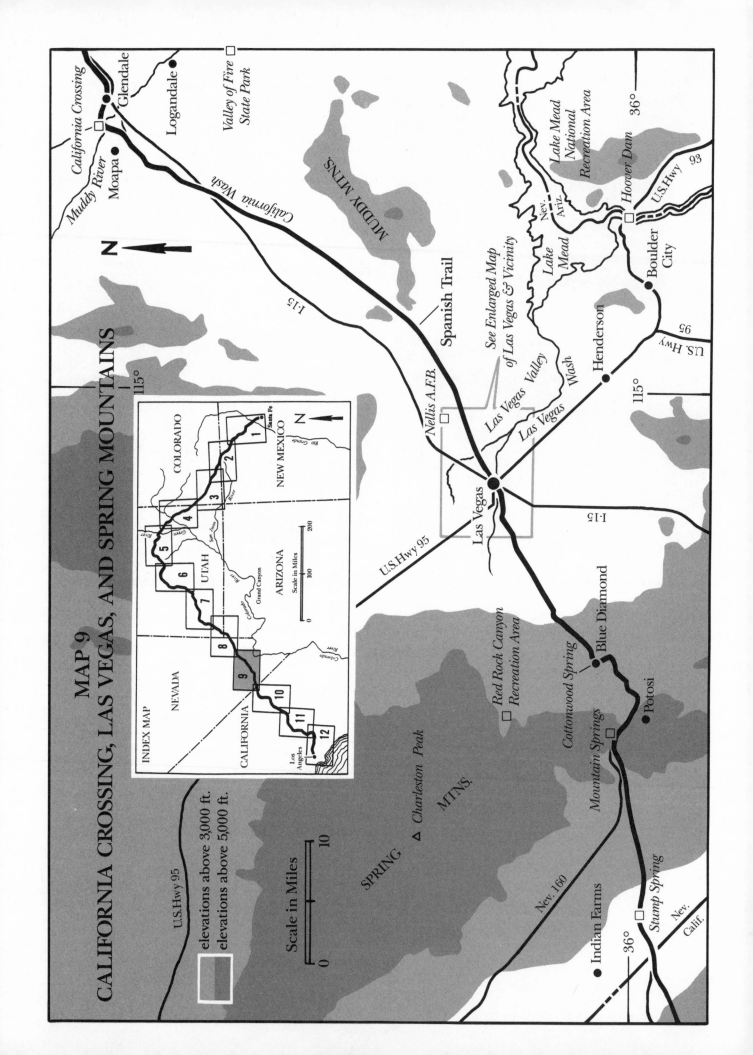

MAP 9
CALIFORNIA CROSSING, LAS VEGAS, AND SPRING MOUNTAINS

elevations above 3,000 ft.
elevations above 5,000 ft.

Scale in Miles
0   10

U.S.Hwy 95

California Crossing
Glendale
Logandale
Muddy River
Moapa
Valley of Fire
State Park

N

California Wash

MUDDY MTNS

I-15

Spanish Trail

Nellis A.F.B.

See Enlarged Map
of Las Vegas & Vicinity

Lake Mead National
Recreation Area

Hoover Dam   36°

U.S.Hwy 93

Lake
Mead

Nev.
Ariz.

Boulder
City

Henderson

Las Vegas Valley

Las Vegas
Wash

Las Vegas

Las Vegas

115°

U.S. Hwy
95

I-15

U.S.Hwy 95

Red Rock Canyon
Recreation Area

Cottonwood Spring

Blue Diamond

Mountain Springs

Potosi

SPRING

MTNS.

△ Charleston Peak

Nev. 160

Indian Farms

Stump Spring

Nev.
Calif.

36°

INDEX MAP

COLORADO

NEW MEXICO

Santa Fe

Rio Grande

Rio Grande

N

1
2
3
4
5
6
7
8
9
10
11
12

NEVADA

UTAH

ARIZONA

CALIFORNIA

Green River

San Juan River

Colorado River

Grand Canyon

Colorado River

Los Angeles

Scale in Miles
0   100   200

LEFT: *Waterwheel on the Muddy River near Glendale, still in use in 1947. Traveling the Spanish Trail in 1848, Orville Pratt thought that the valley of the Muddy would support a large population in the future.*
BUREAU OF RECLAMATION

ABOVE: *Moapa on the Muddy, a settlement near the California Crossing on the Spanish Trail.*

CHAPTER IX

CALIFORNIA CROSSING, LAS VEGAS, AND SPRING MOUNTAINS

From California Crossing on the Muddy River, the Spanish Trail traverses open desert to the springs and meadows at Las Vegas, the best water hole on the entire route, where the modern metropolis thrives. Beyond the historic oasis, the trail climbs the Spring Mountains and descends over a long slope to reach the California border.

CALIFORNIA CROSSING

In the Moapa Valley, two miles west of Glendale, the Spanish Trail crosses the Muddy River to the mouth of California Wash. Orville Pratt and party arrived here on October 10, 1848, and made a "delightful camp" on what was already known as the Muddy. It was a "fine steam of water with good grass" and we "found a large body of Indians—Piutes," he wrote. "From them we bought some green corn and beans. And what a meal we made!"

After a good meal, Pratt went on to praise the valley of the Muddy with its fertile lands and the "best and purest kind" of water. Some day, he thought, "this valley will teem with a large & healthy population."[1] Given Pratt's good words about the Muddy, one wishes that Frémont's melodious name for the river—"Rio

---

[1] *Pratt (1954), 355.*

ALL PHOTOS THIS PAGE: *On Meadow Valley Wash, a tributary of the Muddy, are located remarkable petroglyphs probably made by Paiute Indians after seeing horsemen riding the Spanish Trail.* BELOW: S. K. MADSEN

de los Angeles"—could have been saved.

The Muddy crossing is often referred to in the literature as the "Old California Crossing," a name post-dating 1848. From this point forward, the word "California" appears here and there in the nomenclature of the trail, a word of hope, or optimism, given by wagon drivers pulling across long desert *jornadas* (*jornada:* a day's march) leading to the promised land.

LOST CITY AND VALLEY OF FIRE

Modern highways follow the old trails. Interstate 15 touches the Spanish Trail at Parowan Valley, Mesquite, Mormon Mesa, California Crossing, Las Vegas, Cajon Pass. As Americans embraced the automobile following World War I, road building scarcely kept pace with the demands of a nation on wheels. States and sections cooperated in des-

ignating sea-to-sea highways and "trails," and associations and automobile clubs supported road building and publicized attractions and facilities along the routes. During the twenties, over a dozen such major roads appeared on the map. One of these was the Arrowhead Trail—Salt Lake City, Las Vegas, Los Angeles—a new name for the "old California Road," or the "Mormon Road," which we identify with the Spanish Trail beyond Parowan Valley.

The Arrowhead Trail followed the Spanish Trail in some places and diverged from it in others. The original Arrowhead passed through St. Thomas (inundated by Lake Mead) in the Lower Moapa Valley near "Lost City," an extensive Anasazi ruin being excavated in the 1920s. Much was made of Lost City in the promotional literature plumping the attractions along the Arrowhead Trail.

Replicas of Anasazi buildings on the grounds of Lost City Museum, Overton.

Readers of this book, following the Spanish Trail, may wish to visit the Lost City Museum at Overton on Lake Mead, and the nearby Valley of Fire, Nevada's oldest state park, both of which are located several miles south of the trail. The museum, a state institution, displays artifacts from the Lost City, also known as Pueblo Grande de Nevada, inundated by the rising waters of Lake Mead during the construction of Hoover Dam. Typical buildings from the site have been reconstructed on the grounds of the museum. The exhibits also acquaint the visitor with some of the material culture of the native Paiute Indians whose small reservation is located on the Muddy, three miles above California Crossing.

Valley of Fire derives its name from the brilliant red and orange sandstone formations. Prehistoric man hunted and gathered food here and left inscriptions in many places. Indeed, some of the best examples of rock art in southern Nevada may be seen here. Sections of the old Arrowhead Trail have been preserved and are easily visited.

Exhibits at the visitor center illustrate regional geology, ecology, prehistory, and history.[2]

THE LONG *JORNADA*

From California Crossing, caravans on the Spanish Trail faced a long, waterless *jornada* of over 50 miles to Las Vegas. The route follows up the wide California Wash for 27 miles and then crosses broken country for about 12 miles to the present site of Nellis Air Force Base, on the edge of Las Vegas Valley.

This exceedingly dry desert was one of the most difficult places on the Spanish Trail for

---

[2] *Crampton (1976), 120-122.*

87

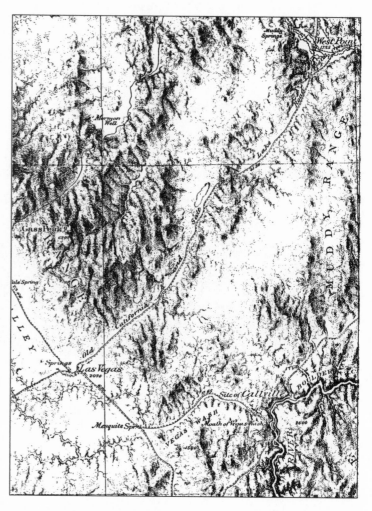

BELOW: *Valley of Fire, a Nevada state park, was on the Arrowhead Trail—opened in the 1920s—which paralleled the Spanish Trail.*

both men and animals. Starting across this stretch on May 4, 1844, Frémont counted the skeletons of horses. He wrote in his journal that it was a "dry *jornada*, which proved the longest we had made in our journey—between fifty and sixty miles without a drop of water."[3]

For those in wagons coming along later, the crossing was even more difficult. Solomon N. Carvalho in 1854 noted:

> We passed a number of deserted wagons on the road; chairs, tables, bedsteads, and every article of housekeeping, were strewn along our path. The emigrant party who had preceded us about ten days, from Parowan, to lighten their wagons, threw out first one article and then another, until everything they had was left on the road. It was not difficult to follow their trail; in one hour I counted the putrid carcasses of nineteen oxen, cows, mules and horses; what a lesson to those who travel over

such a country, unadvised and unprepared.[4]

A mile or two beyond Nellis, the tired mules, horses, and oxen smelled water and made a beeline for the meadows—*las vegas*—watered by Las Vegas Springs.

Right here, let us praise the work of Sherwin "Scoop" Garside and John Lytle, two Las Vegas businessmen who carried out an elaborate program of marking the Spanish Trail across Nevada. This was conceived as a means of celebrating Nevada's Centennial in 1964. After researching the location of the trail, and investigating the terrain through which it passed, the two men, with the support of others, including the Sea Explorer Scouts, placed thirty-eight, 200-pound white, concrete pylons at important places along the

[3] *Jackson and Spence, eds. (1970), I, 686.*
[4] *Korn, ed. (1954), 295.*

Section of the Spanish Trail near Nellis Air Force Base. S. K. MADSEN

In 1964, concrete markers were placed at locations along the Spanish Trail in Nevada. One of these was placed near Interstate 15 overlooking California Wash.

trail. These Centennial Markers are still in place and may be seen by interested travelers today. One pylon, off Interstate 15 (Exit 80, north side of freeway), overlooks California Wash.

LAS VEGAS: "THE DIAMOND OF THE DESERT"

Boiling up with force enough to keep a man from sinking, Las Vegas Springs was the largest spring watering hole on the Spanish Trail. Its importance is shown by the personal accounts of travelers. Frémont describes the springs on May 3, 1844: "Two narrow streams of clear water, four or five feet deep, gush suddenly, with a quick current, from two singularly large springs; ...The taste of the water is good, but rather too warm to be agreeable; the temperature being 71° in the one, and 73° in the other. They, however, afforded a delightful bathing place."[5]

Here emigrant parties rested, enjoyed the pure waters, and some of them discarded their unneeded baggage. Addison Pratt of the Jefferson Hunt wagon train observed that the discarded items included "clothing and featherbeds; there were piles of goose feathers and down lying in heaps."[6]

Solomon N. Carvalho on November 30, 1854, wrote that it was a large spring about "forty-five feet in diameter." It contained "the clearest and purest water I ever tasted." One member of the party, bathing in the spring, reported that he could not sink.

Hardly believing it possible that a man could not sink in fresh water, I undressed and jumped in. What were my delight and astonishment, to find all my efforts to sink were futile. I raised my body out of the

[5] *Jackson and Spence, eds. (1970), I, 685-686.*
[6] *Hafen and Hafen, eds. Journals of Forty-Niners (1954a), 91.*

89

ABOVE: *The Mormon Fort, or Las Vegas Ranch, on the Spanish Trail is the oldest building in Las Vegas.* S. K. Madsen

RIGHT: *Bronze plaque in Lion's Club Park where some of the Meadows—the original vegas—have been preserved.*

THE OLD SPANISH TRAIL
1829 – 1850
STRETCHING FOR 130 MILES ACROSS CLARK COUNTY, THIS HISTORIC HORSE TRAIL BECAME NEVADA'S FIRST ROUTE OF COMMERCE IN 1829 WHEN TRADE WAS INITIATED BETWEEN SANTA FE AND LOS ANGELES. THE TRAIL WAS LATER USED BY THE WAGONS OF THE "49ERS" AND MORMON PIONEERS. CONCRETE POSTS MARKING THE TRAIL WERE ERECTED IN 1965.
NEVADA HISTORICAL MARKER NO. 52

water, and suddenly lowered myself, but I bounced upwards as if I had struck a springing-board. I walked about in the water up to my arm-pits, just the same as if I had been walking on dry land.

Others of the party jumped in. Carvalho tells us: "Twenty-three men were at one time bobbing up and down in it endeavoring to sink, without success." Carvalho continues: "If it were not for this 'blessed water,' it would be almost impossible for man to travel across these deserts."[7]

Gwinn Harris Heap of the Beale Survey describes Las Vegas: "This oasis deserves the name of The Diamond of the Desert, so beautiful and bright does it appear in the centre of the dreary waste that surrounds it."[8]

Waters from the springs, forming a creek about three feet wide and fifteen inches deep, flowed through a shallow channel for three miles and then spread out over the floor of Las Vegas Valley, giving life to meadows measuring two and one-half miles long by half a mile wide, according to two Mormon observers on the spot in 1855. There was grass here—plenty of it—and abundant water. Near at hand, there was a forest of mesquite to supply travelers a hard firewood as good as coal. This was one of the best camping places on the Spanish Trail, especially appreciated by the wagon trains pulling through here after 1848. To reach the springs from the meadows, the Spanish Trail kept to the north of Las Vegas Creek. From the springs, where many parties camped, the trail headed southwest across the open desert.

Of this oasis on the Spanish Trail, there's not much to see now. The springs have been capped to help supply the city's water needs.

[7] *Korn, ed. (1954), 296-297.*
[8] *Heap (1957), 240.*

ABOVE: *Lorenzi Park, home of the Nevada State Museum and the Nevada Historical Society.*

LEFT: *The bright lights of Fremont Street, Las Vegas.*
LAS VEGAS NEWS BUREAU

The creek bed has been rechanneled or covered over with concrete. But, at least some of the meadow lands have been preserved in Lion's Club Park, a splendid grassy place of ample acres with shaded picnic areas and a playground. A commemorative plaque marks this as one of the major stopping places on the Spanish Trail.

We can, with fair approximation, trace the Spanish Trail through the burgeoning Las Vegas, the largest city on the trail between Santa Fe and the outskirts of Los Angeles. A good starting place is the Las Vegas Ranch, also known as the "Mormon Fort," at Las Vegas Boulevard North and Washington Avenue. The building you see here, the oldest in Las Vegas, is the remnant of the fort begun in 1855 by the Mormons, the first settlers in the valley. Later owners, O. D. Gass and Helen Stewart, developed the place into a working ranch.

The Mormons selected a site for their structure on the creek at the head of the meadows, a favorite camping place for trail riders. Thus, from the old ranch, now a museum open to the public, we can follow the Spanish Trail across Las Vegas Boulevard (at 831.096 miles from Santa Fe!). Then, staying to the north of the creek, the trail parallels Bonanza Road and the Las Vegas Expressway to Valley View Boulevard, near the Meadows Mall. The Las Vegas Springs are now hidden inside the fences of the Las Vegas Water District compound bordering Valley View Boulevard. No monument or plaque marks the location of these historic springs.

Near the corner of Valley View Boulevard and Washington Avenue, about a mile from the site of Las Vegas Springs, you will find the Nevada State Museum and the Nevada Historical Society, housed in a delightful facility

ABOVE LEFT: *Tourist photographs Spanish Trail marker in the village of Blue Diamond, watered by Cottonwood Spring.*

ABOVE: *The Spanish Trail crossed the Spring Mountains Range west of Blue Diamond.*

LEFT: *Highway marker between Blue Diamond and Mountain Springs.*

at Lorenzi Park. These agencies are charged with the collection, preservation, and exhibition of materials relating to the history and natural history of the state. The society has collections of manuscripts, books, photographs, maps, and artifacts. It publishes the *Nevada Historical Society Quarterly*. Students of Spanish Trail history, or the traveler following the trail, will find much of interest in the museum galleries and the library collections. A gift shop offers a wide range of novelties, books, and guides.

The special collections department in the James R. Dickinson Library, University of Nevada Las Vegas, on Maryland Parkway, affords rich research in Nevada and regional history.

COTTONWOOD SPRING

From the Las Vegas Springs, the trail heads southwest to reach Cottonwood Spring at Blue Diamond, a distance of about 16 miles over not very difficult terrain. For several miles beyond Las Vegas Springs, we cannot follow the Spanish Trail precisely, since it has been obliterated by urban development and construction. One such real estate development, a resort community not far from the old trail, has chosen the name "Spanish Trail."

On the trail to Cottonwood Spring and beyond, we have at hand a study by the Nevada Office of the Bureau of Land Management, *Archaeology of the Old Spanish Trail/Mormon Road from Las Vegas, Nevada to the California Border* by Keith Myhrer, William G. White, and Stanton D. Rolf (1990). After background research, archaeologists Myhrer and Rolf walked that portion of the trail not covered by highway, from the outskirts of Las Vegas to the California border.

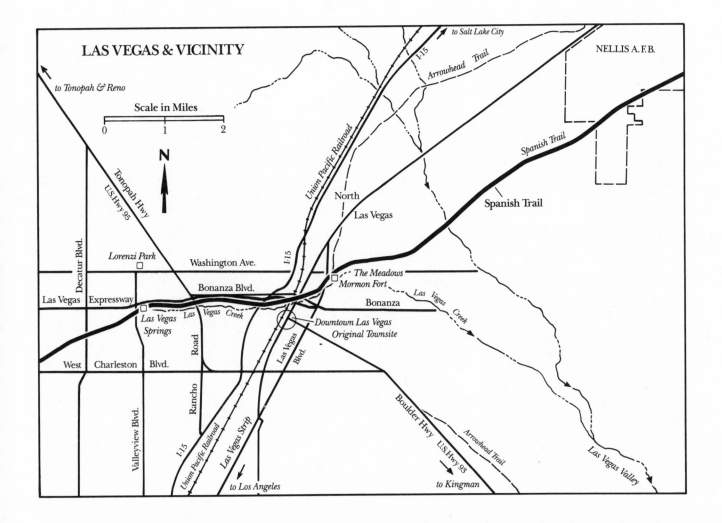

LAS VEGAS & VICINITY

From an assemblage of artifacts gathered along the way, the authors identified a route used primarily as a wagon road from the 1880s to the first decade of the twentieth century. The wagon road paralleled the Spanish Trail and was in places coterminous with it.

Cottonwood Spring, in the center of the village of Blue Diamond, was an adequate camping place on the Spanish Trail. Frémont found good grass here in sufficient quantity and an abundance of water in holes. Later travelers write of good feed and water.

Atlas Sheet No. 66, published by the Wheeler Survey, illustrates the findings of that agency's expeditions of 1869, 1872, and 1873, and is a good guide for us to the "Old California and Salt Lake Road" from Beaver Dam, Arizona, to Resting Springs in California. We have determined that Wheeler's "road" is in many places coterminous with the

Spanish Trail. One such section is the road from Las Vegas to Cottonwood Spring.[9]

MOUNTAIN SPRINGS

From Blue Diamond, the Spanish Trail, by way of a sandy, rocky stream bed, quickly climbs to Mountain Springs Summit of the Spring Mountains range. At an elevation of 5,502 feet, this is the highest point reached by the trail in Nevada. Just beyond the summit, the trail reaches Mountain Springs. Here, Carvalho writes of the clear, cold water nestled in the "bosom of these mountains."[10] Nevada highway markers at the summit will serve as a reminder that you are traveling on the Spanish Trail.

The Potosi lead-silver-zinc mine on Potosi

[9] Map, Wheeler (1869-1873).
[10] Korn, ed. (1954), 297.

Mountain, about five miles south of the Spanish Trail on Mountain Springs Summit, was the earliest mining camp in southern Nevada, opened in 1856. The name comes to us from the fabulously rich sixteenth-century mining town discovered by the Spaniards in colonial Peru, now Bolivia. The fact that the Potosi mine was close to the Spanish Trail probably gave rise to the legend that Potosi Mountain had been discovered and worked by Spaniards in the sixteenth century. When it was reported that rich silver ore had been found at Potosi, there was something of a mining rush to the spot by California prospectors who were always on the lookout for big bonanzas in the interior West. According to reports, prospectors still search Potosi Mountain for evidence of legendary Spanish mines.

If prospectors rushed over the Spanish Trail to Potosi, Nevada, they did so elsewhere as well. All along the Spanish Trail, from New Mexico to California, "lost mines" ascribed to Spanish discoverers have popped up. Since Spain did discover so many big bonanzas in South and North America, the popular mind assumes that wherever Spaniards trod, they must have found rich mines of silver and gold. And so, they took the Spanish Trail to look for them.

STUMP SPRING

From Mountain Springs, the Spanish Trail follows a southwesterly course for about 20 miles to Stump Spring. For approximately five miles below the summit, the trail drops some 1,300 feet; it then follows a gentle slope to the spring. At five miles from the summit, the Kingston cutoff left the Spanish Trail to rejoin it later (see Silurian Lake).

ABOVE: *Two markers at Mountain Springs Summit commemorate the Spanish Trail.*

RIGHT: *On the Spanish Trail looking north and east across Pahrump Valley to the Spring Mountains Range.*

Standing alone, open on every side with nothing growing nearby but low desert brush, the Stump Spring site, on the eastern side of the broad Pahrump Valley, was a somewhat uncertain water source. Frémont on April 30, 1844, noted that the "grass was nearly as scarce as water." Orville Pratt, October 14, 1848, refers to this spring as "Escarbado." Gwinn Harris Heap, August 13, 1853, calls it "Aqua Escarbada." (Spanish *escarbar:* to dig or scratch. That is, water obtained by digging.)[11] In recent times, the spring, in the bottom of a wash in a most bleak environment, has been used as a water source for grazing animals.

At two miles from Stump Spring, the Spanish Trail crosses the Nevada-California border at 879.596 miles from Santa Fe.

---

[11] *Jackson and Spence, eds. (1970), I 684; Pratt (1954), 356; and Heap (1957), 242.*

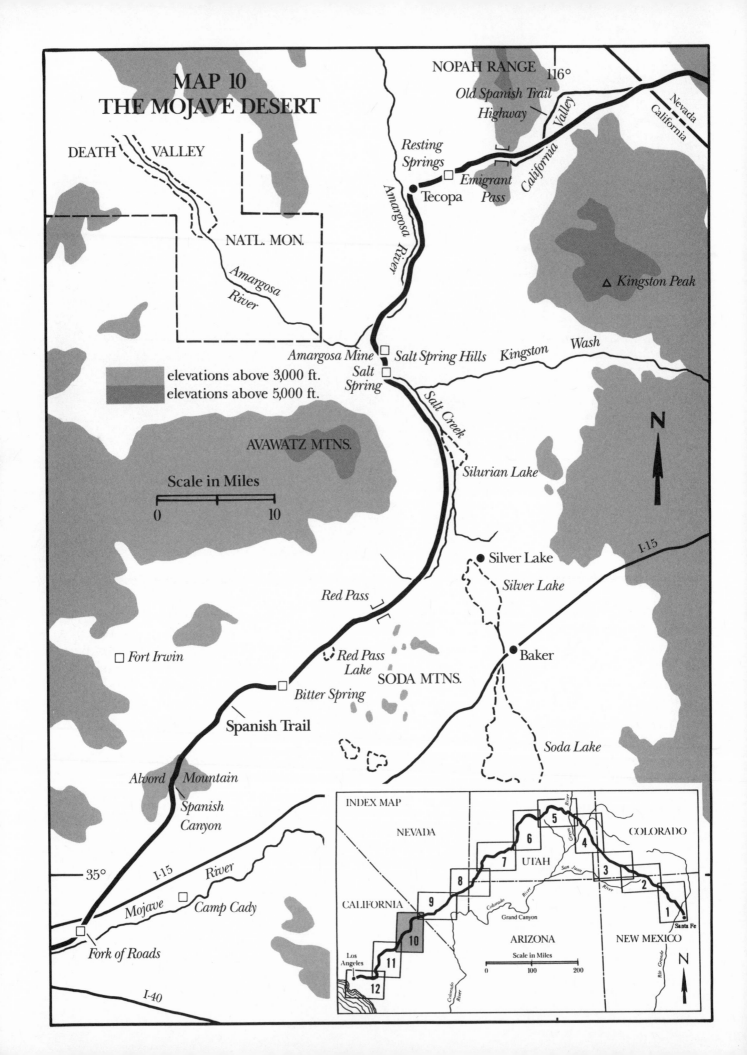

MAP 10
THE MOJAVE DESERT

DEATH VALLEY

NOPAH RANGE 116°

Old Spanish Trail Highway

Resting Springs

NATL. MON.

Amargosa River

Emigrant Pass

□ Tecopa

California Valley

Nevada California

△ *Kingston Peak*

elevations above 3,000 ft.
elevations above 5,000 ft.

Amargosa Mine □ *Salt Spring Hills*
□ *Salt Spring*

Kingston Wash

Salt Creek

AVAWATZ MTNS.

Silurian Lake

N

Scale in Miles

0   10

● Silver Lake

Silver Lake

I-15

Red Pass

□ *Fort Irwin*

Red Pass Lake

SODA MTNS.

● Baker

□ *Bitter Spring*

Spanish Trail

Soda Lake

Alvord Mountain

Spanish Canyon

35°   I-15   *River*

Mojave □ *Camp Cady*

□

Fork of Roads

I-40

INDEX MAP

NEVADA

COLORADO

5
6
4
UTAH
7
3
8
2
CALIFORNIA
9
1
Santa Fe
10
Grand Canyon
11
Los Angeles
ARIZONA
NEW MEXICO
12
Colorado River
San Juan River
Green River
Rio Grande

Scale in Miles
0   100   200

N

Cactus and yucca plants highlight the desert environment of California Valley.

CHAPTER X

THE MOJAVE DESERT

From the California line, the Spanish Trail cut across the heart of the Mojave Desert. The route was largely determined by the infrequent watering places, most of which were of marginal quality, at best. Resting Springs, Salt Spring (near Death Valley National Monument), and Bitter Spring are focal points on the trail and in the region's history.

CALIFORNIA VALLEY

From the California line, the Spanish Trail follows a west southwest course across Pahrump Valley to a low divide separating it from California Valley, bounded on the west by the Nopah Range. Standing on this low divide, near one of the Nevada Centennial markers, one may look back to the east for a splendid view of the Spring Mountains in the distance. Caravans found little difficulty crossing this stretch of approximately 12 miles, though there was no water to be had.

In California Valley, the modern "Old Spanish Trail Highway" (from the California line to Tecopa) commemorates the trail.

EMIGRANT PASS

From the nearly level California Valley, travelers were forced to climb a steep trail to reach Emigrant Pass on the Nopah Range.

Old Spanish Trail Highway stretching across California Valley.

The Spanish Trail at Emigrant Pass in the Nopah Range is clearly visible today.

After reaching the pass, Gwinn Harris Heap of the Beale Survey, in 1853, commented on the "magnificent, but solemn and dreary view" obtainable from the top. Since the Old Spanish Trail Highway crosses the pass, present-day motorists may enjoy the same view. At the crest, Heap commented: "The solitude was unrelieved by the song of bird or the chirp of insect; the mournful murmur of the breeze, as it swept over the desert, was the only sound that broke the silence. In many places, a deceptive mirage spread fictitious lakes and spectral groves to our view, which a puff of wind, or a change in our position, suddenly dissolved."[1] Heap's solitude today is broken only by the occasional car rolling along the Old Spanish Trail Highway. On the western side of Emigrant Pass, just past the summit in a gulch to the right, the original Spanish Trail may still be seen from the highway.

RESTING SPRINGS

From Emigrant Pass, the Spanish Trail drops down six miles to Resting Springs, a historic watering place from the trail days to the present time. This was known as "Archilette" Spring, but Frémont renamed it "*Agua de Hernandez*—Hernandez's Spring" when he arrived to find that Paiute Indians had killed two Mexicans, Santiago Giacome and one Hernandez. Two women in their party had been carried away. The only survivor on the scene was a lap dog. This was a tragic end of a story which began six days earlier on the Mojave River.

We must recall that Frémont and party were traveling the Spanish Trail from west to east. At the Mojave River, Frémont had met two survivors of the massacre, Andreas Fuentes and a boy, Pablo Hernandez, who

[1] *Heap (1957), 242.*

98

ABOVE: *General view of Resting Springs.*
S. K. MADSEN

LEFT: *The Spanish Trail on the Western slope of Emigrant Pass.*

had escaped with a band of horses, which they had left at Bitter Spring, Frémont's "Agua de Tomaso." The next day, Frémont's party reached Bitter Spring to find that the horses had been driven off by the Indians. At this point, Kit Carson and Alex Godey volunteered to chase the marauders and recover the herd. In the afternoon of the next day, with a war whoop, Carson and Godey rode into camp with a band of horses. They had found the Indian encampment and recovered the animals. "Two bloody scalps dangling from the end of Godey's gun announced they had overtaken the Indians as well as the horses," Frémont wrote. After this episode, reminiscent of the literature of violence of the old West, Frémont's party rode on to Resting Springs where they saw the grisly remains of the massacre and the lap dog.

In his report, Frémont praised Carson and Godey for their bold recovery of the stolen horses from the "robbers of the desert." Frémont's words were enough to launch Carson on a life of exploits across the Southwest.

The massacre, and the events leading up to it, are extensively covered by Frémont in his report for the days April 24-29, 1844. He was so consumed with interest in these events that he became careless with routes, mileages, and campsite locations, and his map between the Mojave River and Stump Spring is somewhat inaccurate.[2]

Resting Springs was the best camping ground on the Spanish Trail between Mountain Springs and the Mojave River. Parley P. Pratt wrote on May 21, 1851:

We are now encamped at a place called Resting Springs. Where we arrived on the

[2] *Jackson and Spence, eds. (1970), I, 676-684.*

LEFT: *Ranch buildings among the trees at Resting Springs.*

BELOW: *Tecopa's business section fronts the Old Spanish Trail Highway (1974).*

19th after dark. This is a fine place for rest and recruiting Animals, being a meadow of rich grass, and sufficiently extensive to sustain thousands of cattle. . . .Since Leaving the vegas we have traveled 75 m. s. [w.] through a most horrable desert. Consisting of mountains, Ridges, and plains of Naked Rock, or Sand and Gravel and Sometimes Clay, destitute of Soil or fertility.[3]

Beyond Resting Springs, now a ranch in private ownership, the Spanish Trail crosses open desert for several miles to reach Tecopa.

AMARGOSA RIVER

Tecopa, in the heart of the Amargosa country, once a station on the now defunct Tonopah and Tidewater Railroad, stands at the head of a shallow canyon of the Amargosa River through which the Spanish Trail passes. Tecopa's main street was dedicated in 1974 as the Old Spanish Trail Highway, the western terminus of which is a mile or two outside of town.

The Amargosa (Spanish: bitter) River is an eccentric and capricious stream, flowing underground almost as much as it flows on the surface. In 1853, G. H. Heap described the canyon of the Amargosa as "a ravine containing a scanty supply of warm, fetid, and nauseating water, in a succession of holes."[4] Dr. Thomas Flint on December 2, 1853, said the river water was so impregnated with alkali that "the men did not need soap to wash their greasy shirts in it."[5]

Of the Amargosa, Addison Pratt on November 30, 1849, said:

[It] is a grand curiosity, there is quite a stream about knee deep and so strongly

---

[3] *Stanley and Camp, eds. (1935), 66.*
[4] *Heap (1957), 243.*
[5] *Westergaard, ed. (1923), 66.*

The trail followed down the bed of the Amargosa River.

impregnated with alkali that it is about the color of madeira wine and is said to kill cattle when they drink it, in many places grass is plenty and good, the banks or walls on each side appear to be composition of clay lime and saleratus and in many places presents the appearance of dilapidated walls of ancient castles and other works of art and among these lives an abundance of conies and in the brush a plenty of quails.[6]

Inhabiting the Amargosa's narrow, steep-walled gorge today are over 200 bird species and some invertebrates protected by the Amargosa River Canyon Preserve of the Nature Conservancy. For about 12 miles, the Spanish Trail follows down the Amargosa, then leaving the stream, swings to the south to reach the Salt Spring Hills.

DEATH VALLEY NATIONAL MONUMENT

Near the point where the Spanish Trail leaves the Amargosa River, it reaches the lowest point between Santa Fe and Cajon Pass— 420 feet above sea level. In this section, the trail passes within five miles of Death Valley National Monument, created in 1933. Death Valley is the lowest, hottest, driest desert in North America, and certainly one of the most beautiful. The valley is bordered by the lofty Panamint Range on the west. From Bad Water at 279.8 feet below sea level, the valley's low point, you may view Telescope Peak, elevation 11,049 feet in the Panamint Range, the monument's highest point.

Let us now return to the Jefferson Hunt Monument on the Spanish Trail near Newcastle, Utah. The story of the Forty-niners who left the Spanish Trail and found themselves in Death Valley is well known. Those luckless emigrants managed to cross

[6] *Hafen and Hafen, eds. (1954a), 95.*

ABOVE: *The Spanish Trail left the Amargosa just below the mouth of the river's shallow canyon.*

LEFT: *Tecopa. Passing the time of day.*

the valley in its middle reaches. One party, the Harry Wade family, found a way out by turning south to reach the Spanish Trail on the Mojave River near Barstow.[7]

Students of the Spanish Trail will profit by a visit to Death Valley's well-designed visitor center museum, for a good orientation to the natural and historic points of interest in and near the monument. A wide variety of regional publications is available at the information desk.

SALT SPRING-AMARGOSA MINE

Gold on the Spanish Trail, 1849. On December 1, 1849, Addison Pratt and three others of the Jefferson Hunt wagon train discovered gold in a vein of quartz running through a granite formation in a narrow canyon in the Salt Spring Hills, on the Spanish Trail, five miles from the Amargosa

River. While the California-bound Forty-niners were trying to get out of Death Valley, and while many gold-seekers were heading for California by way of the Spanish Trail, it remained for Addison Pratt, a Mormon missionary bound for the South Seas, to make this important discovery of the precious metal. Pratt recognized the gold-bearing rock, since he had already been to the California mines after returning from his first mission to the South Seas.

When it became known in Los Angeles that the Jefferson Hunt party had discovered gold on the Spanish Trail, there was a small rush to the "Mormon diggin's" early in 1850. One of those early on the scene was Andrew Sublette of the famous trapping family. Lode mining began, as one outfit after another searched for the big bonanza. Sporadic Indian

[7] *Lingenfelter (1986), 40, 47-49.*

The Spanish Trail ran near the southern boundary of Death Valley National Monument.

attacks complicated mining operations. If you follow the Spanish Trail today through the narrow half-mile-long canyon, you will see the remains of extensive mining. As early as 1853, Gwinn Harris Heap of the Beale Survey noted that:

> ...Much to our surprise, we discovered the remains of houses, *rastres* (*arrastras:* Mexican quartz crushers), and all the appliances of gold mining. These, we subsequently ascertained, were the Salt Spring Gold Mines, where a fortune had been sunk by men who were sufficiently deluded or sanguine to abandon the rich mines of California, travel across one hundred and fifty miles of desert, and live upwards of twelve months in a spot so desolate and forlorn that there is actually not sufficient vegetation to keep a goat from starvation.[8]

A spring in the mining area was developed and produced water of fair quality. Some writers have identified this with Salt Spring, which is located half a mile away on Salt Creek, a southern tributary of the Amargosa. Hence, the name Salt Creek Mines. Amargosa, which does appear in the literature, would be a better name for the mines.

Salt Spring consists of ground water forced to the surface by underlying bedrock. A flow of water on the surface may continue for some distance, and it is through this area that the Spanish Trail crossed. The spring is well named. David G. Thompson, of the U.S. Geological Survey, writes in 1929 that the water contains a very high concentration of sodium chloride.

In desert folklore, this spring has been called "poisonous," but W. C. Mendenhall, writing for the U.S. Geological Survey in 1909, states that these waters do not contain

[8]*Heap (1957), 244.*

Salt Spring Hills where gold was discovered on the Spanish Trail in 1849. Salt Creek is the thin line of green near the base of the hills. S. K. MADSEN

arsenic, and are not poisonous. However, they do "contain very large amounts of sodium and magnesium sulphates, being in fact an almost saturated solution of Glauber and Epsom salts. Men delirious from thirst, whose sense of taste is nearly lost, may easily drink so heartily of these waters as to produce fatal results."[9]

In late April 1844, Frémont said that this was "a swampy, salty spot, with a little long, unwholesome grass; and the water, which rose in springs, being useful only to wet the mouth, but entirely too salt[y] to drink. All around was sand and rocks, and skeletons of horses which had not been able to find support for their lives."[10]

We examined Salt Creek where the Spanish Trail crosses it. Frémont's description in 1844 accurately fits the place today. We found a small stream of salty water flow-ing along through heavy stands of cattails and tamarisk. The water was not unpleasant to the taste.

SILURIAN VALLEY

From Salt Spring, the Spanish Trail follows up Salt Creek nine miles to Silurian Lake, a dry white playa about two and one-half miles long, in Silurian Valley.

Here we must mention a cutoff from the Spanish Trail, that started about five miles below Mountain Springs in Nevada and, by way of Kingston Spring, followed a general southwest and west southwest direction to reach the main trail at Silurian Lake. According to early travelers, this route, identified on some maps as the "mail route," saved

---

[9] *Thompson (1929), 605-606; and Mendenhall (1909), 48-49.*

[10] *Jackson and Spence, eds. (1970), I, 682.*

Abandoned buildings at the Amargosa gold mine.

as much as 40 miles, though it was a difficult passage at best.[11]

In 1854, Solomon Carvalho found the Kingston route to be bad enough that, nearing the end of the cutoff, he said: "This was decidedly the worst ground I had ever travelled." Furthermore, he said, *I never want to traverse it again.*"

On this trail, Carvalho met Thomas L. "Peg-leg" Smith, mountain man and teller of tall tales, traveling in a party of ten men, all mounted on mules. The party had been on a prospecting trip to the Colorado River and was now heading for Los Angeles. Carvalho described Peg-leg as "a weather-beaten old chap."[12]

We must add that the Kingston route was a cutoff, used by wagon trains, post-dating 1848. We have made no attempt to follow this cutoff.

We note that the township plats, reflecting U.S. government land surveys covering the Silurian Lake area, carry the notation, "Salt Lake Road 1856." These, or similar notations, are found on the township plats covering the Spanish Trail all the way from Cajon Pass to the California-Nevada boundary, and beyond. These notations were made by the General Land Office surveyors, establishing baselines and meridians across southern California in the 1850s. In carrying out their duties, the surveyors mapped existing roads, and we find, in many instances, that they are following the route we identify as the Spanish Trail. In fact, in some problematical sections, we have used these surveyors' notations to identify the Spanish Trail. We note the names of S. C. Wiltse, A. H. Jones,

[11] *Map, Custer (1861).*
[12] *Korn, ed. (1954), 300-301.*

ABOVE: *The crumbling ruins of the Silver Lake station on the Tonopah and Tidewater Railroad, as they appeared in 1978.*

RIGHT: *Salt Spring at the crossing of the Spanish Trail.*

William Denton, and Henry Washington, whose surveys were made 1855-1857.

From Silurian Lake, the Spanish Trail makes a big swing south and southwest around the base of the Avawatz Mountains to Red Pass. Silver Lake, not far from the Spanish Trail in this area, was a railroad station on the old Tonopah and Tidewater, and was something of a crossroads point for desert travelers at the turn of the century. Some adobe ruins mark the spot today.

We must say that this stretch of the Spanish Trail is remote and isolated from the world at large. Travelers in this open area will find themselves deep in the Mojave Desert, far from centers of population.

BITTER SPRING

From Red Pass, the Spanish Trail takes a southwesterly course for about 11 miles, skirting the normally dry Red Pass Lake on its north side, to reach Bitter Spring, a historic watering hole in the heart of the Mojave Desert.

Near the head of a long wash that drains southeastward to West Cronise Lake, the spring emerges at a point where the wash narrows in a somewhat clayey area. David G. Thompson, of the U.S. Geological Survey, writes in 1929 that the water is of "poor quality. The high sulphate content gives it the bitter taste from which its name is derived. Nevertheless it can be used in an emergency."[13]

The number of travelers who write of the spring, attest to its importance as a vital water hole. John C. Frémont, the first visitor of whom we have record, named it "Agua de Tomaso," corrupted by some later writers to

[13] *Thompson (1929), 546.*

The dry playa of Silurian Lake.
S. K. Madsen

"Agua de Tio Mesa," and other variants. "There were a few bushes and very little grass," Frémont wrote, but "its water was cool—a great refreshment to us under a burning sun."[14]

Since Bitter Spring was the first sure water after Salt Spring, or even Resting Springs, travelers welcomed the water, despite its poor taste. Let us cite here a few accounts from people coming along in wagons. Dr. Thomas Flint, on December 6, 1853, said the water was very bitter, but "it answered very well when made into tea and could be drank clear by not stopping to taste it."[15]

Gwinn Harris Heap, on August 16, 1853, describes the hardship crossing the *jornada* from Salt Spring with the Beale expedition: The heat was almost unbearable. Their guns became almost too hot to touch, and the wind, laden with sand, blew in their faces.

The mules grew weaker, and the men were forced to trudge along on foot. "After twenty hours of continuous march, completely prostrated with heat, toil, hunger, and thirst,...we reached the Agua del Tio Meso." The spring water was "barely drinkable." The grass was "scanty and salt; but when mules are starving, they are not particular in their choice of food." Heap calls this oasis a "wretched spot," but he admitted it was the only resting place between the Amargosa and the Mojave River.

Heap gives us this fiction about the old Mexican, Meso, styled *Tio*, or uncle, who found this spring when his party was nearly perishing from thirst. The party celebrated, and Uncle Meso rambled about the place until he fell dead from apoplexy. Two peons in

[14] *Jackson and Spence, eds. (1970), I, 679.*
[15] *Westergaard, ed. (1923), 67.*

The waters of Bitter Spring flow through a tangle of cattails and tamarisk. S. K. MADSEN

Marker on the trail at Bitter Spring.

the party died of starvation, and the next travelers who came along found their skeletons locked together "as if they had expired in the act of devouring one another." Heap identifies Agua del Tio Meso with Frémont's Agua de Tomaso, and some later writers have confounded the two and even moved one or the other to different locations.[16]

Carvalho's account of June 3, 1854, gives us some details: "At noon we arrived at Bitter Springs, the grounds about which are strewn with dead animals, and the polluted atmosphere at this time, one o'clock, P.M., ranges at 95° in the shade of our wagons, and is nearly unbearable. This is a howling, barren wilderness; not a single tree or shrub for the last fifty miles, nor is there one in sight now. I did not observe during the last day's travel a lizard or any sign of animal or insect life."[17]

Bitter Spring figures in the "Paiute War"

of 1860, when Indians attacked traders on the Salt Lake Road, i.e., the Spanish Trail. The army sent Major James Henry Carleton to campaign against them and to stabilize the frontier. Carleton scoured the desert from the Mojave River to Death Valley to Las Vegas. He established a command post at Camp Cady on the Mojave River, and three redoubts at strategic places, one at Bitter Spring. After a few skirmishes in the field, some Paiutes came into Camp Cady for peace talks. Following this, Carleton abandoned Camp Cady and the redoubts and returned to the coast.[18] The redoubt at Bitter Spring is now just a mound of clay on a small bluff, west of the spring.

During our investigations, we found the

---

[16] *Heap (1957), 244-246.*
[17] *Korn, ed. (1954), 302.*
[18] *Casebier (1972).*

The Spanish Trail in Alvord Mountain.

spring water quite palatable, though warm, with a slight soda taste, but not noticeably bitter. The spring water flows as far as a quarter of a mile from its source. The waters support much plant life, including prolific stands of tamarisk and cattails, interspersed with mesquite trees. In walking about the spring area, we noted some evidence of mining equipment.

Bitter Spring is not easy to reach. Twenty-one miles of the Spanish Trail, including Bitter Spring, lies within the Fort Irwin Military Reservation, the National Training Center for the United States Army Forces Command. Here, the army engages in highly sophisticated and realistic combat training. Security is tight, and permission is required for entrance to the reservation. Thus, in tracing the Spanish Trail through this sector, we relied on the road marked out by the town-

ship surveyors in 1855-1856.

We mention now the important work of the U.S. Geological Survey in mapping and describing the watering places in the Mojave Desert. Detailed logs of routes leading to these watering spots were published in papers appearing between 1909 and 1929, at a time when development of the Mojave was beginning with some intensity. In a paper published in 1921 by David G. Thompson, two routes to Bitter Spring are described.[19] Of course, this was some time before the closure of some of the area by the United States Army.

These works, highly useful to us, gave suggestions for desert travel at a time when the automobile was just coming of age. In following the Spanish Trail, we have crossed many areas where desert travel is still hazardous. A sampling: dry washes of bottomless

[19] *Thompson (1921), 214, 216-217.*

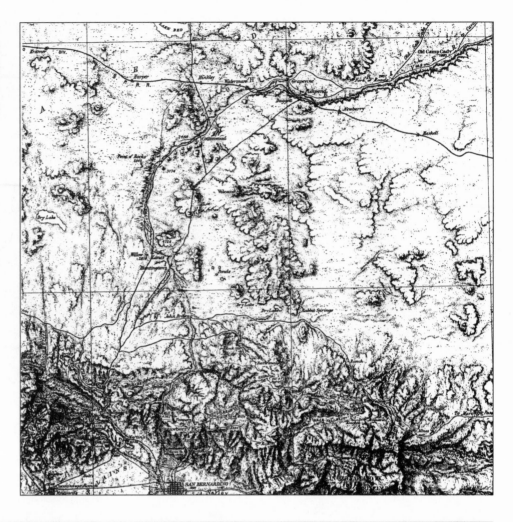

Section of Atlas Sheet No. 73 of the Wheeler Survey issued in 1883 shows "Fork of the Roads" and the desert country above Barstow (Grapevine) to Cajon Pass.

NATIONAL ARCHIVES

sand become rivers of quicksand after a heavy rain. Water is scarce today in many places, as it was in the Spanish Trail days. Sand storms will remove the paint from a vehicle. Sharp rocks may pierce an oil pan or a six-ply tire. Many back roads are unmarked; some don't appear on any map. The desert can be a dangerous place.

From Bitter Spring, the Spanish Trail follows a southwesterly course to the foot of Alvord Mountain, where it leaves today's military reservation. The trail passes over the mountain, a vast granitic pile, by way of Spanish Canyon, also called Mule Canyon, and then continues on the same course across open desert to the "Fork of Roads" at the Mojave River. Thence, it continues upstream to cross the river at the present city of Barstow. Many travelers on the Spanish Trail, leaving the tortuous desert behind them, gave thanks when they reached the waters of the Mojave River.

The "Fork of Roads" shown on Atlas Sheet no. 73 of the Wheeler Survey, is a historic spot where two main trails crossing the Southwest come together. The "Old Salt Lake Road" is shown, which is, of course, the Spanish Trail.[20] The other, the "Mojave Trail" or "Mojave Road," not identified as such by Wheeler, comes in here from New Mexico and Fort Mohave on the Colorado River. The actual Fork of Roads is in an open area four miles east of Yermo, just south of Interstate 15.

[20] *Map, Wheeler (1883).*

Ruins of Camp Cady on the Mojave River, where water was near the surface, was established to protect desert travelers from Indian raids.
PHOTO BY GLENN EDGERTON IN DESERT TREASURE, HEFFERNAN, RICHARDS, SALISBURY (1939).

CHAPTER XI

BARSTOW, MOJAVE RIVER, AND THE APPROACH TO CAJON PASS

The Spanish Trail reaches the Mojave River near modern-day Barstow, a crossroads of the Mojave Desert. With water at hand, and the California coast not far away, trail riders continued up the tree-lined river to a point near Victorville and, at a quickened pace, started up the long slope leading to Cajon Pass.

BARSTOW

Barstow, on the Mojave River, is a major crossroads city in the Mojave Desert. Trails and wagon roads crossed here and, as traffic increased in time, we may note that the Union Pacific and Santa Fe railroads, as well as Interstates 15 and 40, come together here.[1]

The intrepid Franciscan, Father Francisco Garcés, opened the Mojave Trail when he traversed the desert from the Colorado River to San Gabriel in 1776. Garcés passed along this section of the Mojave River, which he called "River of the Martyrs," in March 1776. Elliott Coues, who edited the Garcés diary, reminds us that in 1865, as a member of a military expedition, he followed Garcés' trail. On the Mojave River, at about nine miles below the

[1] *Hart (1978). Guidebooks have formed an important source in our trail research. The extensive work by Hoover, Rensch, and Rensch (1966) is a basic work.*

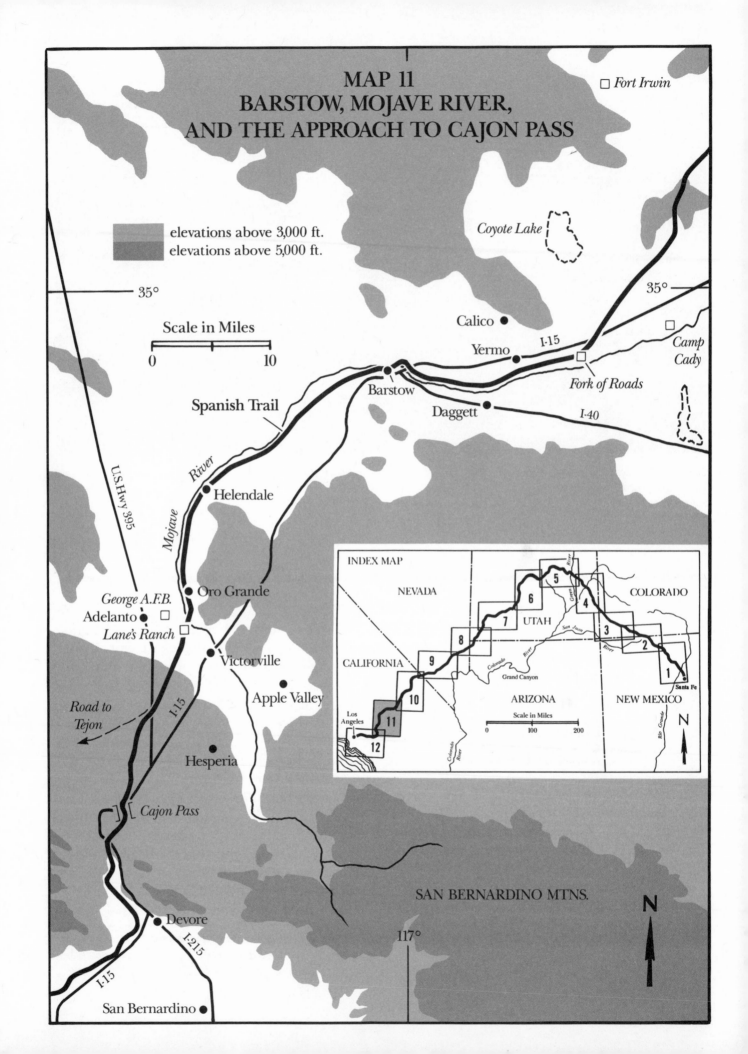

MAP 11
BARSTOW, MOJAVE RIVER,
AND THE APPROACH TO CAJON PASS

□ *Fort Irwin*

elevations above 3,000 ft.
elevations above 5,000 ft.

35°   35°

Coyote Lake

Scale in Miles

0   10

Calico ●

Yermo ●   I-15   □   *Camp Cady*

Barstow   Fork of Roads

Spanish Trail

Daggett ●   I-40

River

Helendale ●

Mojave

Oro Grande ●

George A.F.B.
Adelanto ● □
Lane's Ranch □

Victorville ●

Apple Valley ●

Road to Tejon   I-15

Hesperia ●

Cajon Pass

U.S.Hwy 395

SAN BERNARDINO MTNS.   N

Devore ●   I-215

I-15

San Bernardino ●

INDEX MAP

NEVADA   5
6   COLORADO
7   UTAH   4
8   3
9   2
CALIFORNIA   Grand Canyon   1
10   Santa Fe
Los Angeles   ARIZONA   NEW MEXICO
11   Scale in Miles
12   0   100   200   N

117°

ABOVE: Casa del Desierto, *the Santa Fe Railroad station and Harvey House at Barstow.*

LEFT: *Classification yard of the Santa Fe Railroad at Barstow.*

Fork of Roads, he came upon Camp Cady, which had been reactivated after Carleton's time. He says of this place on November 4, 1865: What a "God-forsaken Botany Bay of a place, the meanest I ever saw yet for a military station, where four officers and a handful of men manage to exist in some unexplained way in mud and brush hovels."[2] Although nine miles from the Spanish Trail, Camp Cady was the headquarters for the Carleton military campaigns in the post-trail period.

Lieutenant A. W. Whipple, who had been commissioned by the War Department in 1853 to locate a railroad route along the thirty-fifth parallel, reached the Spanish Trail at the Fork of Roads on March 13, 1854. He called it the "Mormon" Road and noted fresh wagon tracks leading towards Salt Lake City. The Whipple Survey was one of the federal Pacific Railroad Surveys of which the

Gunnison Expedition, noted earlier, was one.[3]

Beyond Barstow, information about the Spanish Trail is literally buried beneath the accounts of traders, prospectors, freighters, emigrants, government explorers, federal troops, and railroad, highway and freeway builders. Still, as elsewhere, some of these late-comers knew they were following the Spanish Trail. Thus, the information they provide will help us identify accurately the route of the old trail all the way to Cajon Pass, and beyond.

At Barstow, the Bureau of Land Management operates the "California Desert Information Center," a well-designed facility housing exhibits and displays about the natural and cultural history of the High Desert, that is, the Mojave Desert, from Death Valley to

[2] *Coues (1900), I, 242.*
[3] *Foreman, ed. (1941), 263-264.*

The Bureau of Land Management's "California Desert Information Center" at Barstow.

Cajon Pass. The BLM publishes a detailed map of the region. Descriptive brochures and specific desert travel information are also available.

The Mojave River Valley Museum, in Barstow, seeks to preserve and interpret the historical and natural heritage of the valley, and maintains a museum emphasizing valley history. As a bicentennial project, the museum association published *Once Upon a Desert*, a detailed history of the Mojave Desert, from the time of Francisco Garcés to 1976, when the book was published. Price, $17.76.[4]

MOJAVE RIVER

From Barstow, the Spanish Trail follows up the Mojave River close to the right, or east, bank, to a point near Oro Grande, where it crosses the river and heads for Cajon Pass.

A typical desert river, the Mojave rises in the high San Bernardino Mountains and, as it flows out onto the desert plain, much of the water sinks into its sandy bed so that, in its lower reaches, it is dry much of the time. During extreme floods, the bed may fill with water and even reach the "sink of the Mojave," many miles to the east of Barstow. However, the river's water seldom reaches the surface at Barstow.

Following the Spanish Trail, Frémont describes the stream some distance below the crossing at Oro Grande, northwest of Victorville. He found the river to be a "clear bold stream, 60 feet wide, and several feet deep." It ran between "perfectly naked banks of sand. The eye, however, is somewhat relieved by willows, and the beautiful green of the sweet cottonwoods with which it is well wooded." Frémont gave us the name

[4] *Keeling, ed. (1976).*

The Mojave River at Lane's Crossing.
S. K. MADSEN

"Mohahve River," a spelling which happily has been lost to time.[5]

We get some idea about the road up the Mojave from Lieutenant A. W. Whipple's account in March 1854. The stream was flowing where he crossed it and for 20 miles the land was fertile, but grass was scarce. The road, he said, was excellent, and as he continued the ascent, the river grew larger and cottonwood and mesquite trees were more abundant.[6]

At the Spanish Trail crossing of the Mojave River, G. H. Heap observed on August 20, 1853, that the river was "a rapid stream, twenty-five yards in breadth and one foot in depth, but its water was too warm to be drinkable. Passed several fine meadows near the river, and saw bands of antelopes, also hares and partridges."[7]

Posted signs along this stretch tell us now that this was once part of the National Old Trails Highway, one of those "national" highways marked out after World War I. The Arrowhead Trail, which was coterminous with the Spanish Trail in sections of California, Nevada, and Utah, also passed through here. And, let us not forget that this was a part of the fabled federal Route 66, "America's Main Street," a highway for many of those hurt by the Great Depression who sought better times in California.[8]

From the Fork of Roads to the crossing at

---

[5] *Jackson and Spence, eds. (1970), I, 675-676.*
[6] *Foreman, ed. (1941), 264.*
[7] *Heap (1957), 248-249.*
[8] *Route 66 is a part of American history. It became "the main street of America" in the decades after 1932, when it was completed. Kelly (1980) has described the route and its people in modern times. Rittenhouse (1989) has reprinted his guidebook of Route 66, first issued in 1946.*

115

Old building at Turner Ranch at Lane's Crossing.

Oro Grande, the Spanish Trail follows along the Mojave River for approximately 50 miles. The crossing was utilized for years by later travelers. A. G. Lane established a store at "Lane's Crossing," about 1861, to serve wagon traffic.[9] Atlas Sheet No. 73 of the Wheeler Survey, published in 1883, shows a road (essentially the Spanish Trail) all the way from the Fork of Roads to the crossing at "Lanes."[10]

ROAD TO CAJON

From the Mojave River, riders on the Spanish Trail went up a gradual slope heading for the opening between the lofty San Bernardino and San Gabriel mountains—Cajon Pass. En route, they passed through a forest of Giant Joshua, indicating the western side of the Mojave Desert.

On his second expedition, Frémont left the central valley of California and, following the Tejon Pass, struck the Spanish Trail below the Cajon summit, some 13 miles from the Mojave River. The "pathfinder" had hoped to find the Spanish Trail and follow it on his return to the East. On April 20, 1844, he writes: "After a difficult march of 18 miles, a general shout announced that we had struck the object of our search—THE SPANISH TRAIL—which here was running directly north." Frémont, traveling from west to east, has been our guide all along the trail to Paragonah, Utah, where he left it.[11] He gives us some good accounts of life and conditions

[9] *Peirson (1970), 137-138. Beattie and Beattie (1951) have written a scholarly treatise on the San Bernardino country. Their work includes much information on the Mojave Desert roads and trails.*
[10] *Map, Wheeler (1883).*
[11] *Jackson and Spence, eds. (1970), I, 674.*

ABOVE: *Explorers of the Spanish Trail break for lunch on the road to Cajon Pass.*

LEFT: *New Mexican trader.* BREWERTON, OVERLAND WITH KIT CARSON, (VINTON, ED.)

along the trail; but it is George Brewerton, traveling with Kit Carson in 1848, who provides an excellent description of a Spanish Trail caravan:

"We finally overtook and passed this party, after some eight days' travel in the Desert." Their appearance was striking.

Imagine upward of two hundred Mexicans dressed in every variety of costume, from the embroidered jacket of the wealthy Californian, with its silver bell-shaped buttons, to the scanty habiliments of the skin-clad Indian, and you may form some faint idea of their dress. Their caballada contained not only horses and mules, but here and there a stray burro...destined to pack wood across the rugged hills of New Mexico. The line of march of this strange cavalcade occupied an extent of more than a mile. . . .

Many of these people had no fire-arms, being only provided with the short bow and arrows usually carried by New Mexican herdsmen. Others were armed with old English muskets. . . .

Near this...crowd we sojourned for one night; and passing through their camp after dark, I was struck with its picturesque appearance. Their pack-saddles and bales had been taken off and carefully piled, so as not only to protect them from damp, but to form a sort of barricade or fort for their owner. From one side to the other of these little corrals of goods a Mexican blanket was stretched, under which the trader lay smoking his cigarrito, while his Mexican servant ...prepared his coffee and 'atole.'[12]

---

[12] *Vinton, ed. (1930), 58-60.*

117

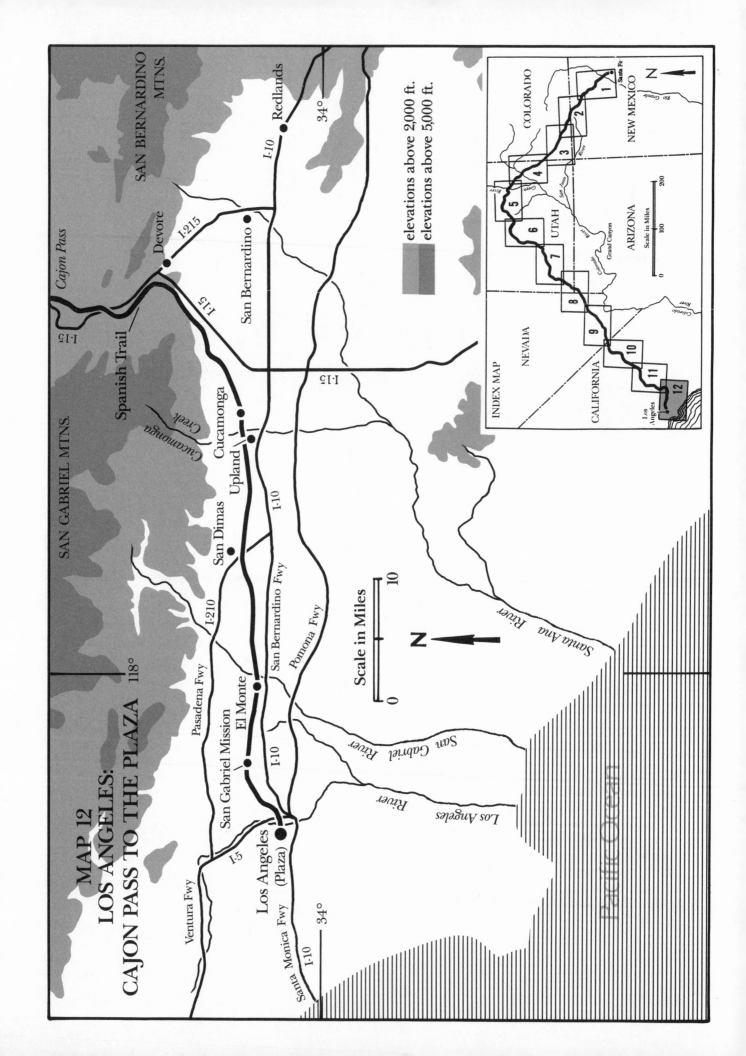

MAP 12
LOS ANGELES:
CAJON PASS TO THE PLAZA

Scale in Miles

elevations above 2,000 ft.
elevations above 5,000 ft.

INDEX MAP

COLORADO

NEW MEXICO

Santa Fe

Rio Grande

N

Scale in Miles

200

100

0

UTAH

ARIZONA

Grand Canyon

Green River

San Juan River

Colorado River

NEVADA

CALIFORNIA

Colorado River

Los Angeles

SAN BERNARDINO MTNS.

SAN GABRIEL MTNS.

Cajon Pass

Spanish Trail

Cucamonga Creek

Devore

Redlands

San Bernardino

Cucamonga

Upland

San Dimas

El Monte

San Gabriel Mission

Los Angeles (Plaza)

Pasadena Fwy

I-210

Ventura Fwy

I-5

Santa Monica Fwy

I-10

San Bernardino Fwy

Pomona Fwy

I-10

I-10

I-15

I-215

I-15

I-15

I-10

34°

34°

118°

San Gabriel River

Los Angeles River

Santa Ana River

Pacific Ocean

ABOVE LEFT: *The head of the Spanish Trail at the summit of Cajon Pass.* S. K. MADSEN

LEFT: *The Spanish Trail-Brown's Toll Road at the head of Crowder Canyon.*

CHAPTER XII

LOS ANGELES: CAJON PASS TO THE PLAZA

At Cajon Pass, riders on the Spanish Trail left behind the harsh Mojave Desert as they descended to the gentle environment of the Los Angeles coastal basin. Not far from the base of the pass, the caravan traders reached Cucamonga, the first Spanish settlement they had seen since leaving New Mexico. Trail's end was the Los Angeles Plaza, now the center of a vast metropolis.

CAJON PASS

From the interior deserts, Cajon Pass is a historic gateway to the coastal region of southern California. Opened by desert Indians, developed by Spanish explorers, fur traders, and the New Mexico-California caravans, the pass today accommodates trains and speeding automobiles on Interstate 15. In earlier years, many of those who moved slowly along on horseback, or in wagons, expressed deep appreciation as they left the desert behind and entered the broad cultivated valleys and meadows, and the balmy weather, of the Los Angeles Basin.

The Cajon summit consists of a ridge or rim several miles in length. It is easily approachable from the desert side on the north, but on the southern side, which drains into Cajon Creek and Cajon Canyon, it is steep and rough. The Spanish Trail reaches

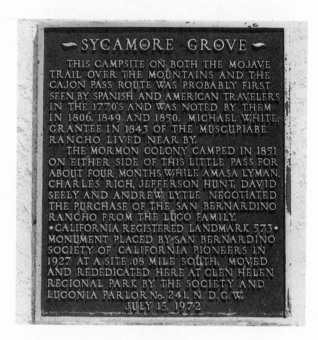

LEFT AND BOTTOM LEFT: *"Santa Fe and Salt Lake Trail" monument at the Sullivan-May Center in Cajon Canyon.*

BELOW: *Plaque describes the history of Sycamore Grove.*

the summit (elevation 4,200 feet above sea level) very near Interstate 15 and descends rapidly, for about half a mile. The trail then drops into Crowder Canyon, a tributary of Cajon Creek, and follows it to its mouth in the main Cajon Canyon. Crowder is a modern name for Coyote Canyon. The lower two miles of the canyon, narrow, steep and rough, was known in pioneer times as the "Upper Narrows." We note here that the original township plat, covering the mouth of Crowder Canyon, describes this section as the "Spanish Trail 1855-6."

To avoid the steep Spanish Trail, other routes across the Cajon summit area were developed to accommodate wagons. One of these, the "Salt Lake Road 1855-6," opened by William Sanford, was much used by the Mormons to reach their settlement at San Bernardino. Another was the John

Brown Toll Road, opened in 1861, which generally paralleled the Spanish Trail and passed through Crowder Canyon. A monument commemorating the later explorers and traders who followed the "Santa Fe & Salt Lake Trail" stands near the mouth of Crowder Canyon. A similar monument may be seen nearby, at the Sullivan-May Nature Center and Historic Site, a facility of the San Bernardino County Museum.[1]

From Crowder, the Spanish Trail follows down the narrow Cajon Canyon, today crowded with railroad tracks and highways, to the Glen Helen Regional Park near Devore. This is a historic spot. Father Francisco Garcés came this way on March 22, 1776. The American fur trapper, Jedediah Smith, passed through here in 1826 and again in 1827. Mormon colonists camped here at

[1] *Haenzel (1976).*

ABOVE: *The winery at Cucamonga.*

RIGHT: *"Madonna of the Trail" monument at Upland on the Spanish Trail.*

Sycamore Grove in 1851 before locating on the Rancho San Bernardino. Lieutenant Whipple came through here with his railroad survey in 1854. It was here that the Spanish Trail turned westward toward Los Angeles.

CUCAMONGA

From Sycamore Grove, at the mouth of Cajon Canyon, the Spanish Trail, passing through vineyards and meadows with herds of grazing cattle and horses, followed a west-southwest direction for about 14 miles to the Rancho Cucamonga, a Mexican land grant established in 1839. This must have been a welcome sight for the riders on the Spanish Trail, since this was the first white settlement they had encountered after leaving Abiquiu in New Mexico. The distance from Santa Fe was 1,082.155 miles.

Camped under a wide-spreading oak at the rancho on New Year's Eve, 1850, David W. Cheesman describes his feelings. The major-domo had presented his party with fresh beef: "None but the half-famished can tell of the joy this gave us for we had had but little fresh meat since we left Salt Lake and none for the last four hundred miles of travel." Chickens crowing was "music to our ears. . . .We had now arrived in the Valley of California. The mountains, dreary wastes and deserts were behind us. Here opened up the most lovely country we had ever beheld. The grass was up and seemingly all over the valley, some four inches in height, the climate soft and exhilarating."[2]

About this time, other writers found exhilaration in the wine, one of the products of the rancho located amidst vineyards on every side. Today's winery at the rancho claims

[2] *Foy, ed. (1930), 302.*

ABOVE: *One panel of the "Madonna of the Trail" monument commemorates the explorations of Jedediah Smith.*

RIGHT: *The bell tower of Mission San Gabriel.*

1839 as its founding date. Most of those writing about the rancho, in the early days, tripped over its spelling. Examples: Kokomungo, Cucumonga, Coco Mongo, Comingo, Chocomonga, Gomingo.

Orville Pratt, who had traveled the Spanish Trail all the way from Santa Fe, and whose diary has helped us in many places, arrived at the ranch on October 23, 1848. Here he got the first news of the discovery of gold at Sutter's Mill, and he could scarcely believe his ears. Some men were making as high as fifty dollars a day in the gold placers![3] News of the gold discovery spread rapidly, and the whole world rushed in. We have mentioned a few of the many Forty-niners who chose to follow the Spanish Trail to California.

Two miles west of Cucamonga, on Euclid Avenue at Foothill Boulevard in Upland, and

right on the Spanish Trail, there appears a "Madonna of the Trail" monument, erected by the Daughters of the American Revolution, one of a series marking the National Old Trails Road. A plaque on one of the stores in downtown Upland commemorates the "Santa Fe Trail." We have encountered this usage along the Spanish Trail at a number of places. It should be said that, in historical usage, the Santa Fe Trail, running from the Missouri frontier to Santa Fe, stopped at Santa Fe. The Spanish Trail, in our present usage, ran between Santa Fe and Los Angeles.

SAN GABRIEL

Once travelers left Cucamonga, they were traveling on existing roads. There was no Spanish Trail as such. West of Cucamonga, as

---

[3] *Pratt (1954), 358.*

122

RIGHT: *Animated discussion on Olvera Street, Los Angeles Plaza.*

BELOW: *Mosaic describes the history of Mission San Gabriel.*

late as 1883, when Atlas Sheet No. 73 of the Wheeler Survey was issued,[4] there were only two roads shown leading to El Monte, and San Gabriel to Los Angeles. These old roads are now covered by freeways, boulevards, paved streets, and avenues. Trail study in the metropolis can best be described as futile. However, today's Mission Drive and Mission Road, between Los Angeles, San Gabriel, and El Monte, is certainly coterminous with an old road, and this may very well have been the route followed by many of the caravans from Santa Fe.

Mission San Gabriel Arcàngel, the fourth of the California missions, founded in 1771, was one of the most prosperous in the mission chain. It was noted for its vineyards, olive and orange groves; and it produced food, hides, and supplies in abundance. Located on the direct overland route from Sonora, Mexico, to the Spanish capital of California at Monterey, the mission was a strategic stopping place. In like manner, it was a major supply point on the Spanish Trail for the New Mexican caravans. The mission was in the very heart of pastoral California, and many of the animals driven back on the Spanish Trail were rounded up, legally or otherwise, from the lands of the San Gabriel and other missions and ranchos. After secularization of the missions in 1834, San Gabriel lost its lands, and its economic position was greatly diminished. The church, with its long, side wall, marked by high, oblong windows and a tower supporting six historic bells so reminiscent of the architecture of Moorish Spain, makes it one of the popular tourist destinations in Southern California today.

---

[4] *Map, Wheeler (1883).*

Interior of the Avila Adobe, Olvera Street, Los Angeles.

The plaza, Los Angeles.

LOS ANGELES

From San Gabriel, traders from New Mexico headed for Los Angeles, their major objective, nine miles away. El Pueblo de Nuestra Señora la Reina de los Angeles de la Porciùncula—or Los Angeles for short—was established on September 4, 1781, by four soldiers, twelve settlers, and their families, who settled on a 17,500-acre tract on the orders of Spanish Governor Felipe de Neve. During the Spanish and Mexican periods, the population grew steadily, totalling 1,250 in 1845. Los Angeles was the largest settlement in California when it became part of the United States in 1848.

The plaza is now surrounded by official buildings, commercial establishments, and private dwellings. When laid out in 1818, it was the center of life in the pueblo, and the goal of the traders from New Mexico. The plaza in Los Angeles, by way of the Spanish Trail, is 1,120.249 miles from the plaza in Santa Fe. In its external aspects, Los Angeles was quite similar to Santa Fe of the same period. Both pueblos were built of flat-roofed adobe houses clustering around a central square.

After 1821, during the Mexican period, the pueblo became rich, because the spoils of the missions, following secularization, fell into the hands of local inhabitants. Duflot de Mofras, a Frenchman making an inspection of California for his government in 1841, offers these statistics about the wealth of southern California, concentrated in the pueblo of Los Angeles: "...Within an area of 15 or 20 square leagues, local residents own over 80,000 cattle, 25,000 horses, and 10,000 sheep. Vineyards yield 600 barrels of wine, and an equal amount of brandy; grains, however,

El Parque de Mexico *on the Spanish Trail, Los Angeles.*
S. K. Madsen

contribute less than 3,000 *fanegas*" (1 *fanega:* about 1.6 bushels).[5]

The New Mexican traders disposed of their goods here and in neighboring settlements, and then ranged out for some distance in Southern California to buy, or steal, mules and horses to drive back over the trail to Santa Fe.

The Los Angeles Old Plaza, a historic state park, and environs, where, during the years from 1829 to 1848, New Mexican traders mingled with the local gentry as they bargained, sold and soaked up the ambience of the city, is today a place where tourists come to experience the atmosphere reminiscent of the time of the Spanish Trail days.

[5] *Hafen and Hafen,* Old Spanish Trail *(1954b), 187.*

125

BIBLIOGRAPHY

Adams, Eleanor B. and Angelico Chavez, trans. and eds.
1956   *The Missions of New Mexico, 1776: A Description by Fray Francisco Atanasio Domínguez with other Contemporary Documents.* Albuquerque: University of New Mexico Press.

Akens, Jean.
1987   *Ute Mountain Tribal Park (The Other Mesa Verde).* Moab, Utah: Four Corners Publications.

Averett, Walter R.
1962   *Directory of Southern Nevada Place Names.* Revised ed. Las Vegas, Nevada: Walter R. Averett.

Bailey, Lynn R., ed.
1965   "Lt Sylvester Mowry's Report on His March in 1855 from Salt Lake City to Fort Tejon," *Arizona and the West,* 7 (Winter), 329-346.

Barnes, F. A.
1989   *Hiking the Historic Route of the 1859 Macomb Expedition.* Moab, Utah: Canyon Country Publications.

Bartlett, Richard A.
1962   *Great Surveys of the American West.* Norman: University of Oklahoma Press.

Baxter, John O.
1987   *Las Carneradas: Sheep Trade in New Mexico, 1700-1860.* Albuquerque: University of New Mexico Press.

Beattie, George William, and Helen Pruitt Beattie.
1951   *Heritage of the Valley: San Bernardino's First Century.* Oakland, California: Biobooks.

Beckwith, E. G.
1855   "Report of Explorations for a Route for the Pacific Railroad by Capt. J. W. Gunnison, Topographical Engineers, near the 38th and 39th Parallels of North Latitude, from the Mouth of the Kansas River, Mo. to the Sevier Lake, in the Great Basin," in *Reports of Explorations and Surveys to Ascertain the Most Practical and Economical Route for a Railroad from the Mississippi to the Pacific Ocean...,* II. Washington, D.C.: Beverley Tucker, Printer, 9-114.

Bigler, David L., ed.
1990   *The Gold Discovery Journal of Azariah Smith.* Salt Lake City: University of Utah Press.

Bolton, Herbert E.
1950   *Pageant in the Wilderness: The Story of the Escalante Expedition to the Interior Basin, 1776, Including the Diary and Itinerary of Father Escalante Translated and Annotated.* Salt Lake City: Utah State Historical Society.

Breternitz, David A., Christine Robinson, and G. Timothy Gross, comps.
1986   *Dolores Archaeological Program: Final Synthetic Report.* Denver, Colorado: Bureau of Reclamation Engineering and Research Center.

Brodsly, David.
1981   *L.A. Freeway, An Appreciative Essay.* Berkeley: University of California Press.

Brooks, George R., ed.
1977   *The Southwest Expedition of Jedediah S. Smith: His Personal Account of the Journey to California, 18261827.* Glendale, California: Arthur H. Clark Company.

Brooks, Juanita.
1991   *The Mountain Meadows Massacre.* New Foreword by Jan Shipps. Norman: University of Oklahoma Press.

Camp, Charles L., ed.
1966   *George C. Yount and his Chronicles of the West, Comprising Extracts from his "Memoirs" and from the Orange Clark "Narrative."* Denver, Colorado: Fred A. Rosenstock, Old West Publishing Company.

Carlson, Helen S.
1974   *Nevada Place Names: A Geographical Dictionary.* Reno, Nevada: University of Nevada Press.

Casebier, Dennis G.
1972   *Carleton's Pah-Ute Campaign.* Norco, California: Casebier.

____.
1975   *The Mojave Road.* Norco, California: Tales of the Mojave Road Publishing Company.

Castleton, Kenneth B.
1979   *Petroglyphs and Pictographs of Utah: The South, Central, West and Northwest,* II. Salt Lake City: Utah Museum of Natural History.

Church of Jesus Christ of Latter-day Saints.
1847-1930 History Department. Archives Division. Stake and Ward Manuscript Histories.

____.
1847-1849, Journal History of the Church. August 7, 1847; June 5, 1848; September 17, October 2, 9, 1849;
1931   June 18, 1931.

Cleland, Robert Glass.
1950   *This Reckless Breed of Men; the Trappers and Fur Traders of the Southwest.* New York: Alfred A. Knopf.

Cline, Gloria Griffin.
1963   *Exploring the Great Basin.* Norman: University of Oklahoma Press.

Cook, Sherburne F.
1976   *The Conflict between the California Indian and White Civilization.* Berkeley: University of California Press.

Cottam, Walter P.
1961   "Is Utah Sahara-Bound?" in *Our Renewable Wild Lands—A Challenge.* Salt Lake City: University of Utah Press.

Coues, Elliott.
1900   *On the Trail of a Spanish Pioneer: The Diary and Itinerary of Francisco Garcés (Missionary Priest) in His Travels through Sonora, Arizona, and California, 1775-1776.* 2 vols. New York: Francis P. Harper.

Crampton, C. Gregory.
1976   *The Complete Las Vegas, including Hoover Dam and the Desert Water World of Lake Mead and Lake Mohave together with a Peep at Death Valley and a visit to Zion National Park.* Salt Lake City: Peregrine Smith, Inc.

——.
1979   "Utah's Spanish Trail," *Utah Historical Quarterly,* 47 (Fall), 361-383.

——.
1990   "Green River Crossing," Moab, Utah, *Canyon Legacy,* 5 (Spring), 23-27.

Crampton, C. Gregory, ed.
1971   *Utah Historical Quarterly,* 39 (Spring).

Darrah, W. C., ed.
1948-1949 "Journal of John F. Steward," *Utah Historical Quarterly,* 16-17.

Delaney, Robert W., comp.
1979   *Center of Southwest Studies, Opportunities for Research, Fort Lewis College, Durango.* Durango, Colorado: Basin Reproduction and Printing Company.

——.
1977   *Blue Coats, Red Skins, & Black Gowns: 100 Years of Fort Lewis.* Durango, Colorado: Durango Herald.

Denhardt, Robert Moorman.
1941   "Driving Livestock East from California," *California Historical Society Quarterly,* 20 (December), 341-347.

Dimmock, Charles H.
1859   Dimmock Field Notes, Macomb Expedition of 1859. Library of Congress, Manuscripts Division, Rodgers Family File, Series I, vol. 17 (Miscellany) folder entitled, "San Juan Exploring Expedition Topographical Memoir, ca. 1856-58."

Edwards, E. I.
1969   *The Enduring Desert: A Descriptive Bibliography.* Los Angeles: Ward Ritchie Press.

Egan, Howard R.
1917   *Pioneering the West, 1846 to 1878, Major Howard Egan's Diary.* Richmond, Utah: Howard R. Egan Estate.

Ellis, Florence Hawley.
n.d.   *Twelve Centuries in Northern New Mexico.* N.p.: Ghost Ranch Conference Center.

Ellsworth, S. George, ed.
1990   *The Journals of Addison Pratt.* Salt Lake City: University of Utah Press.

Emory, W. H.
1848   *Notes of a Military Reconnaissance, from Fort Leavenworth, in Missouri, to San Diego, in California, including part of the Arkansas, Del Norte, and Gila Rivers.* (30th Cong., 1st Sess., Ex. Doc. No. 41). Washington, D.C.: Wendell and Benthuysen, Printers.

Ferron, Augustus D.
1873-1880 Township plats and survey notes. U. S. Bureau of Land Management, Salt Lake City. Copies in Recorder's Office, Emery County Courthouse, Castle Dale.

Foreman, Grant, ed.
1941   *A Pathfinder in the Southwest: The Itinerary of Lieutenant A. W. Whipple during his Explorations for a Railway Route from Fort Smith to Los Angeles in the Years 1853 & 1854.* Norman: University of Oklahoma Press.

Foy, Mary E., ed.
1930   "By Ox Team from Salt Lake to Los Angeles, 1850: A Memoir by David W. Cheesman,"
            Historical Society of Southern California, Annual Publications, 14, 270-337.

Galvin, John, ed.
1965   *A Record of Travels in Arizona and California, 1775 & 1776: Fr. Francisco Garcés.* New
            Translation. San Francisco: John Howell.

Gannett, Henry.
1877   "Topographical Report on the Grand River District," in F. V. Hayden, *Ninth Annual Report of
            the United States Geological and Geographical Survey of the Territories embracing Colorado and
            Parts of Adjacent Territories.* Washington, D.C.: Government Printing Office.

Gilbert, Bil.
1985   *Westering Man: The Life of Joseph Walker.* Norman: University of Oklahoma Press.

Gregory, H. E., ed.
1939   "Diary of Almon Harris Thompson," *Utah Historical Quarterly,* 7 (January, April, and July), 3-
            140.

Haenzel, Arda M.
1976   *Historical Cajon Pass: A Self-Guided Driving Tour in Three Parts.* Redlands, California: San
            Bernardino County Museum Association.

Hafen, LeRoy R.
1950   "Armijo's Journal of 1829-30; The Beginning of Trade between New Mexico and California,"
            Colorado Magazine, 27 (April), 120-131.

Hafen, Leroy R., ed.
1946   "Colonel Loring's Expedition across Colorado in 1858," *Colorado Magazine,* 23 (March), 49-76.

Hafen, LeRoy R., and Ann W. Hafen. eds.
1954a   *Journals of Forty-Niners, Salt Lake to Los Angeles. . . .*Glendale, California: Arthur H. Clark
            Company.

———.
1954b   *Old Spanish Trail: Sante Fe to Los Angeles.* Glendale, California: Arthur H. Clark Company.

Hague, Harlan.
1978   *The Road to California: The Search for a Southern Overland Route, 1540-1848.* Glendale,
            California: Arthur H. Clark Company.

Hart, James D.
1978   *A Companion to California.* New York: Oxford University Press.

Hayden, F. V.
1876, 1877, *The United States Geological and Geographical Survey of the Territories embracing Colorado
1878   and Parts of Adjacent Territories.* Annual Reports, 8-10. Washington, D.C.: Government
            Printing Office.

Heap, Gwinn Harris.
1957   *In* LeRoy R. Hafen and Ann W. Hafen, eds. *Central Route to the Pacific by Gwinn Harris Heap
            . . . , 1853-54.* Glendale, California: Arthur H. Clark Company.

Hill, Joseph J.
1921   "The Old Spanish Trail," *Hispanic American Historical Review,* 4 (August), 444-473.

———.
1930   "Spanish and Mexican Exploration and Trade Northwest from New Mexico into the Great Basin," *Utah Historical Quarterly,* 3 (January), 3-23.

Hoffman, John F.
1985   *Arches National Park: An Illustrated Guide.* San Diego, California: Western Recreational Publications.

Hoover, Mildred Brooke, Hero Eugene Rensch, and Ethel Grace Rensch.
1966   *Historic Spots in California.* Revised by William N. Abeloe. Third ed. Stanford, California: Stanford University Press.

Huntington, Oliver B.
1855   "The Elk Mountain Mission," *Utah Genealogical and Historical Magazine,* 4 (1913), 188-200. (Andrew Jenson, ed.)

Hussey, John Adam.
1943   "The New Mexico-California Caravan of 1847-1848," *New Mexico Historical Review,* 18 (January), 1-16.

Ivins, Anthony W.
1924   "Along the Spanish Trail Across Southern Nevada," *Nevada State Journal,* Februrary 17.

Jackson, Donald, and Mary Lee Spence, eds.
1970-1984 *The Expeditions of John Charles Fremont.* Urbana: University of Illinois Press, 4 vols. and map portfolio.

Jackson, W. Turrentine.
1952   *Wagon Roads West: A Study of Federal Road Surveys and Construction in the Trans-Mississippi West, 1846-1869.* Berkeley: University of California Press.

Jenson, Andrew.
1941   *Encyclopedic History of the Church of Jesus Christ of Latter-day Saints.* Salt Lake City: Desert News Publishing Company.

Johnson, Lamont.
1951   "The Spanish Trail," Salt Lake City, *Deseret News,* February 25.

Jorgensen, John L.
1955   "A History of Castle Valley to 1890." Unpublished M.S. thesis, University of Utah, Salt Lake City.

Keeling, Patricia Jernigan, ed.
1976   *Once upon a Desert.* A bicentennial project. Barstow, California: Mojave River Valley Museum Association.

Kelly, Charles.
1939   "On Manly's Trail to Death Valley," *Desert Magazine,* 2 (February) 6-8, 41-43.

Kelly, Susan Croce.
1988   *Route 66: The Highway and Its People.* Photography by Quinta Scott. Norman: University of Oklahoma Press.

Kessell, John L.
1980   *The Missions of New Mexico since 1776.* Albuquerque: University of New Mexico Press.

Kohler, Kenneth Olsen.
1989   *Other Truths Not Guessed.* St George, Utah: Classic Printing Co.

Korn, Bertram Wallace, ed.
1954   *Incidents of Travel and Adventure in the Far West by Solomon Nunes Carvalho.* Philadelphia:
            The Jewish Publication Society of America.

Lange, Frederick, Nancy Mahaney, Joe Ben Wheat, and Mark L. Chenault.
1986   *Yellow Jacket: A Four Corners Anasazi Ceremonial Center.* Boulder: Johnson Books.

Lawrence, Eleanor F.
1930   "The Old Spanish Trail from Santa Fe to California." Unpublished M.A. thesis, University of
            California, Berkeley.

____.

1931   "Mexican Trade between Santa Fe and Los Angeles, 1830-1848," *California Historical Society
            Quarterly,* 10 (March), 27-39.

Leiby, Austin N.
1984   "Borderland Pathfinders: The 1765 Diaries of Juan Maria Antonio de Rivera." Unpublished
            Ph.D. dissertation, Northern Arizona University, Flagstaff.

Leonard, Zenas.
1966   *Narrative of the Adventures of Zenas Leonard.* Clearfield, PA.: D.W. Moore, 1839. Readex
            Microprint ed.

Lingenfelter, Richard E.
1986   *Death Valley & the Amargosa: A Land of Illusion.* Berkeley: University of California Press.

Lisle, Laurie.
1986   *Portrait of an Artist: A Biography of Georgia O'Keeffe.* Revised ed. Albuquerque: University of
            New Mexico Press.

Lister, Robert H., and Florence C. Lister.
1983   *Those who Came Before: Southwestern Archeology in the National Park System.* Foreword by
            Emil W. Haury. Globe, Arizona: Southwest Parks and Monuments Association.

McCarthy, Max Reynolds.
1975   "Patrick Edward Connor and the Military District of Utah: Civil War Operations in Utah and
            Nevada, 1862-1865." Unpublished M.S. thesis, Utah State University, Logan.

Macomb, John N.
1876   *Report of an Exploring Expedition from Santa Fe, New Mexico, to the Junction of the Grand and
            Green Rivers of the Great Colorado of the West, in 1859, with Geological Report by Prof. J. S.
            Newberry.* Washington, D.C.: Government Printing Office.

Madsen, Steven K.
1991   "The Spanish Trail through Canyon Country," Moab, Utah, *Canyon Legacy,* 9 (Spring), 23-29.

____.

1992   "The Spanish Trail through Southwestern Utah." Paper presented at the Mormon History
            Association Annual Conference, St. George, Utah, May 15.

Manly, William Lewis.
1966   *Death Valley in '49.* San Jose: Pacific Tree and Vine Co., 1894. Readex Microprint ed.

Marcy, Randolph B.
1859   *A Handbook for Overland Expeditions. With Maps, Illustrations, and Itineraries of the Principal Routes between the Mississippi and the Pacific.* New York: Harper & Brothers.

Mendenhall, Walter C.
1909   *Some Desert Watering Places in Southeastern California and Southwestern Nevada* (U.S. Geological Survey, Water Supply Paper, 224). Washington, D.C.: Government Printing Office.

Miller, David E., ed.
1976   *The Route of the Domínguez-Escalante Expedition, 1776-77: A Report of Trail Research Conducted under the Auspices of the Domínguez-Escalante State/Federal Bicentennial Committee and the Four Corners Regional Commission.* Salt Lake City: Utah State Historical Society.

Möllhausen, Baldwin.
1969   *Diary of a Journey from the Mississippi to the Coasts of the Pacific with a United States Government Expedition.* Translated by Mrs. Percy Sinnett. London: Longman, Brown, Green, Longmans & Roberts, 1858. 2 vols.; New introduction by Peter A. Fritzell. Reprint ed. New York: Johnson Reprint Corporation.

Morgan, Dale L., ed.
1947   "The Exploration of the Colorado River in 1869," *Utah Historical Quarterly,* 15.

____.
1948-1949 "The Exploration of the Colorado River and the High Plateaus of Utah in 1871-72," *Utah Historical Quarterly,* 16-17.

Murbarger, Nell.
1947   "Old Man of the Desert," *Nevada Magazine,* 3 (November), 5-7, 29.

Myhrer, Keith, William G. White, and Stanton D. Rolfe.
1990   *Contributions to the Study of Cultural Resources: Archaeology of the Old Spanish Trail/Mormon Road from Las Vegas, Nevada to the California Border.* (Bureau of Land Management, Nevada Technical Report 17). Washington, D.C.: Government Printing Office.

Myrick, David F.
1970   *New Mexico's Railroads. A Historical Survey.* Golden, Colorado: Colorado Railroad Museum.

Pack, Arthur Newton.
1979   *We Called It GHOST RANCH.* Abiquiu, New Mexico: Ghost Ranch Conference Center.

Paher, Stanley W.
1971   *Las Vegas, As it Began—As it Grew.* Las Vegas: Nevada Publications.

Palmer, William R.
1949   "Latter-day Saint Pioneers and the Old Spanish Trail," Salt Lake City, *Improvement Era,* 52 (February), 88-89, 113-115.

Parkhill, Forbes.
1965   *The Blazed Trail of Antoine Leroux.* Los Angeles: Westernlore Press.

Pearce, T. M., ed. Assisted by Ina Sizer Cassidy and Helen S. Pearce.
1965   *New Mexico Place Names: A Geographical Dictionary.* Albuquerque: University of New Mexico Press.

Peirson, Erma.
1970   *The Mojave River and Its Valley. . . .*Glendale, California: Arthur H. Clark Company.

Pendleton, Mark A.
1948   "Courage and Daring on the Old Spanish Trail," Salt Lake City, *Improvement Era,* 51
            (February), 88-89, 118.

Perkins, George E.
1947   *Pioneers of the Western Desert: Romance and Tragedy Along the Old Spanish or Mormon Trail
            and Historical Events of the Great West.* Los Angeles: Wetzel Publishing Co., Inc.

Powell, J. W.
1875   *Exploration of the Colorado River of the West and Its Tributaries. Explored in 1869, 1870, 1871,
            and 1872, under the direction of the Secretary of the Smithsonian Institution.* Washington, D.C.:
            Government Printing Office.

Powell, J. W., and G. W. Ingalls.
1874   "Report, Washington, D.C., December 18, 1873," in *Annual Report of the Commissioner of
            Indian Affairs, 1873.* Washington, D.C.: Government Printing Office, 41-74.

Pratt, Orville C.
1954   "Diarist: The Journal of Orville C. Pratt, 1848," in LeRoy R. Hafen and Ann W. Hafen, eds., *Old
            Spanish Trail: Santa Fe to Los Angeles.* Glendale, California: Arthur H. Clark Company.

Price, George F.
1897   "Expedition from Fort Crittenden, Utah Ter., to Fort Mojave, Ariz. Ter.," in *The War of the
            Rebellion: A Compilation of the Official Records of the Union and Confederate Armies.* (U.S.
            55th Cong., 1st Sess., House of Rep., Doc. No. 59, Part 1.). Washington, D.C.: Government
            Printing Office.

Quinn, Ann, comp.
1980   "Historical Landmarks of San Bernardino County," *San Bernardino County Museum
            Association Quarterly,* 28 (Fall and Winter).

Reeder, Ray M.
1966   "The Mormon Trail: A History of the Salt Lake to Los Angeles Route to 1869." Unpublished
            Ph.D. dissertation, Brigham Young University, Provo.

Rice, William B.
1942   "Early Freighting on the Salt Lake-San Bernardino Trail," *Pacific Historical Review,* II (March),
            73-80.

Rittenhouse, Jack D.
1989   *A Guide Book to Highway 66.* Facsimile of 1946 ed. Albuquerque: University of New Mexico Press.

Roe, Frank Gilbert.
1955   *The Indian and the Horse.* Norman: University of Oklahoma Press.

Rollins, James Henry.
1941   Autobiography dictated in 1898. Typescript copy. Manuscript file, Spanish Trail. Utah State
            Historical Society, Salt Lake City.

Rousseau, Mrs. James A.
1958   "Rousseau Diary Across the Desert to California from Salt Lake City to San Bernardino in
            1864," *San Bernardino County Museum Association Quarterly,* 6 (Winter), 1-21.

Schroedl, Alan R.
1979   "The Archaic Inhabitants of the Northern Colorado Plateau," *Utah Historical Quarterly,* 47
            (Fall), 344-360.

Silliman, Bert J.
n.d.   Papers on the Spanish Trail. Utah State Historical Society, Salt Lake City.

Silvey, Frank.
n.d.   *History and Settlement of Northern San Juan County*. Foreword by Becky Walker. N.p.

Smart, William B.
1988   *Old Utah Trails*. Salt Lake City: Utah Geographic Series.

Smith, Duane A.
1991   *Sacred Trust: The Birth and Development of Fort Lewis College*. Niwot, Colorado: University
                Press of Colorado.

Stanley, Reva Holdaway, and Charles L. Camp, eds.
1935   "A Mormon Mission to California in 1851: From the Diary of Parley Parker Pratt," *California
                Historical Society Quarterly*, 14 (March), 59-79.

Swadesh, Frances Leon.
1974   *Los Primeros Pabladores: Hispanic Americans of the Ute Frontier*. Notre Dame: University of
                Notre Dame Press.

1914   "Tales of the Old Santa Fe and Salt Lake Trail to California," Chicago, *The Santa Fe Magazine*,
                8 (March), 22-30.

Tanner, Faun McConkie.
1976   *The Far Country: A Regional History of Moab and LaSal, Utah*. Salt Lake City: Olympus
                Publishing Company.

Thompson, David G.
1921   *Routes to Some Desert Watering Places in the Mohave Desert Region, California* (U.S. Geological
                Survey, Water Supply Paper No. 490-B). Washington, D.C.: Government Printing Office.

____.
1929   *The Mohave Desert Region* (U.S. Geological Survey, Water Supply Paper No. 578). Washington,
                D.C.: Government Printing Office.

U.S. Work Projects Administration.
1940   *New Mexico: A Guide to the Colorful State*. New York: Hastings House.

____.
1941a   *Colorado: A Guide to the Highest State*. New York: Hastings House

____.
1941b   *Utah: A Guide to the State*. New York: Hastings House.

Vandenbusche, Duane, and Duane A. Smith.
1981   *A Land Alone: Colorado's Western Slope*. Boulder, Colorado: Pruitt Publishing Company.

Van Dyke, Walter.
1894   "Overland to Los Angeles, by the Salt Lake Route in 1849," *Historical Society of Southern
                California, Annual Publications*, 3, 76-83.

Vinton, Stallo, ed.
1930   *Overland with Kit Carlson, a Narrative of the Old Spanish Trail in '48, by George Douglas
                Brewerton*. New York: Coward-McCann, Inc.

Walker, Clifford.
1967   "Life and Adventure Along the Mojave River Trail," *San Bernardino County Museum Association Quarterly,* 15 (Fall).

____.
1971   "Opening of the Mojave River Trail," *San Bernardino County Museum Association Quarterly,* 18 (Summer).

____.
1986   *Back Door to California: The Story of the Mojave River Trail.* Edited by Patricia Jernigan Keeling. Barstow, California: Mojave River Valley Museum Association.

Warner, Ted J., ed. Translated by Angelico Chavez.
1976   *The Domínguez-Escalante Journal . . . 1776.* Provo, Utah: Brigham Young University Press.

Warren, Elizabeth von Till.
1974   "Armijo's Trace Revisited: A New Interpretation of the Impact of the Antonio Armijo Route of 1829-1830 on the Development of the Old Spanish Trail." Unpublished M.A. thesis, University of Nevada, Las Vegas.

Weber, David J.
1976   "Mexico's Far Northern Frontier, 1821-1854: Historiography Askew," *Western Historical Quarterly,* 7 (July), 279-293.

____.
1982   *The Mexican Frontier, 1821-1846: The American Southwest under Mexico.* Albuquerque: University of New Mexico Press.

Westergaard, Waldemar, ed.
1923   "Diary of Dr. Thomas Flint: California to Maine and Return, 1851-1855," *Historical Society of Southern California, Annual Publications,* 12. Reprint ed.

Wheeler, George M.
1889   *Report upon United States Geographical Surveys West of the One Hundredth Meridian, in Charge of Capt. Geo. M. Wheeler, Corps of Engineers, U.S. Army, under the direction of the Chief of Engineers, U.S. Army. Vol. I: Geographical Report.* Washington, D.C.: Government Printing Office.

1987   *When Cultures Meet: Remembering San Gabriel Del Yunge Oweenge, Papers from the October 20, 1984, Conference held at San Juan Pueblo, New Mexico.* Santa Fe: Sunstone Press.

Whipple A. W.
1855   "Report of Explorations for a Railway Route, Near the 35th Parallel of North Latitude, from the Mississippi River to the Pacific Ocean," in *Reports of Explorations and Surveys to Ascertain the Most Practical and Economical Route for a Railroad from the Mississippi to the Pacific Ocean. . . .* III. Washington, D.C.: Beverley Tucker, Printer.

Wilson, Iris Higbee.
1965   *William Wolfskill, 1798-1866: Frontier Trapper to California Ranchero.* Glendale, California: Arthur H. Clark Company.

MAP BIBLIOGRAPHY

Beckwith, E. G.
1855a   "Map No. 1. From the Valley of Green River to the Great Salt Lake; from Explorations and Surveys made under the direction of the Hon. Jefferson Davis, Secretary of War," in *Reports of Explorations and Surveys to Ascertain the Most Practical and Economical Route for a Railroad from the Mississippi to the Pacific Ocean. . . .* II. Washington, D.C.: Beverley Tucker, Printer.

____.
1855b   "Map No. 4. From the Coo-che-to-pa Pass to the Wasatch Mountains from Explorations and Surveys made under the direction of the Hon. Jefferson Davis, Secretary of War, by Capt. J. W. Gunnison, Topl. Engrs. assisted by Capt. E. G. Beckwith 3d. Artillery," in *Reports of Explorations and Surveys to Ascertain the Most Practical and Economical Route for a Railroad from the Mississippi to the Pacific Ocean. . . .* II. Washington, D.C.: Beverley Tucker, Printer.

Carleton, J. H.
1859   "Map of the Route from Fort Tejon Cal'a, via Los Angeles to Mountain Meadows, Utah T'y." MS. National Archives, Record Group No. U.S. 324/40.

Custer, H.
1861   "Map No.1. From San Francisco Bay to the Plains of Los Angeles from Explorations and Surveys made under the direction of the Hon. Jefferson Davis, Secretary of War, by Lieut. John G. Parke, Topl. Engrs.," in *Reports of Explorations and Surveys, to Ascertain the Most Practicable and Economical Route for a Railroad from the Mississippi River to the Pacific Ocean . . . in 1853-'56.* (36th Cong., 2nd Sess., Senate Ex. Doc.), XI. Washington, D.C.: George W. Bowman, Printer.

Dimmock, Charles H.
1859   Map of Explorations and Surveys in New Mexico and Utah, made under the Direction of the Hon. John B. Floyd, Secretary of War. MS. National Archives, Record Group No. 77.

____.
1860   *Map of Explorations and Surveys in New Mexico and Utah made under the Direction of the Secretary of War.* [In Macomb's published report, 1876.] Washington, D.C.: Government Printing Office. This map drawn by F. W. von Egloffstein was not published until it appeared in Macomb's report of 1876. Egloffstein issued the map separately in 1864 to capitalize on the market for maps as the Colorado mining districts were being opened.

Frémont, John C.
1845   "Map of an Exploring Expedition to the Rocky Mountains in the Year 1842 and Oregon & North California in the Years 1843-44 by Brevet Capt. J. C. Frémont of the Corps of Topographical Engineers," in *Report of. . . .*Washington, D.C.: Gales and Seaton, Printers.

Froiseth, B. A. M.
1878   *Froiseth's New Sectional & Mineral Map of Utah: Compiled from the latest U.S. Government Surveys and other Authentic Sources.* Second ed., Salt Lake City: Froiseth.

Hayden, F. V.
1877   *United States Geological and Geographical Surveys of the Territories, Geological and Geographical Atlas of Colorado and Portions of Adjacent Territory.* Washington, D.C.: Julius Bien.

Humphrey, B. S.
1878   Topographical Sketch of Part of Western Colorado & Eastern Utah, Showing Route of March [E. H. Ruffner Command, 1878]. MS. National Archives, Record Group No. 77.

Miera y Pacheco, Bernardo.
1970   *Plano Geografico. . .1778.* Chihuahua. Facsimile ed. issued by Yale University Press.

U.S. Bureau of Land Management.
n.d.   Township survey plats of the General Land Office for the states of New Mexico, Colorado, Utah, Arizona, Nevada, California.

U.S. Geological Survey.
1885   Utah, Beaver sheet.

_____.
1886   Nevada-Arizona, St. Thomas sheet.

_____.
1891   Utah, St. George sheet.

U.S. Geological Survey. Topographic Maps.
New Mexico. 7.5 Minute Series (1:31,250).
        Santa Fe (1961), *Tesuque* (1953), *Horcado Ranch* (1953; photorevised, 1977), *Espanola* (1953), *San Juan Pueblo* (1953), *Chili* (1953), *Medanales* (1953), *Abiquiu* (1953), *Cañones,* (1953), *Ghost Ranch* (1953), *Echo Amphitheater* (1953), *Alire* (1953), *Canjilon* (1953), *Navajo Peak* (1953), *Cement Lake* (1963), *John Mills Lake* (1963), *Wirt Canyon* (1963), *Carracas Canyon* (1963).

New Mexico. 15 Minute Series (1:62,500).
        Tierra Amarilla (1955), *Boulder Lake* (1955).

Colorado. 7.5 Minute Series (1:31,250).
        Carracas (1954; photorevised, 1971), *Allison* (1954; photorevised, 1971), *Tiffany* (1968), *Ignacio* (1968), *Gem Village* (1968), *Loma Linda* (1968), *Basin Mountain* (1968), *Durango West* (1963), *Hesperus* (1963), *Thompson Park* (1963), *Mancos* (1965), *Millwood* (1965), *Dolores East* (1965), *Dolores West* (1965), *Arriola* (1965), *Yellow Jacket* (1965), *Pleasant View* (1965), *Cahone* (1965), *Cedar 3 NW* (1957), *Dove Creek* (1964).

Colorado. 15 Minute Series (1:62,500).
        Pagosa Junction (1957), *Eastland* (1957).

Utah. 7.5 Minute Series (1:31,250).
        Desert (1969), *Beckwith Peak SW* (1953), *Dry Mesa* (1969), *Chimney Rock* (1969), *Bob Hill Knoll* (1969), *Buckhorn Reservoir* (1969), *Hadden Holes* (1969), *Horn Silver Gulch* (1969), *Emery 1 NE* (1953), *Emery East* (1968), *Walker Flat* (1968), *Old Woman Plateau* (1968), *Yogo Creek* (1966), *Water Hollow Ridge* (1966), *Steves Mtn.* (1966), *Salina* (1966), *Aurora* (1966), *Sigurd* (1966), *Johns Peak* (1968), *Hilgard Mtn.* (1968), *Forsyth Reservoir* (1968), *Fish Lake* (1968), *Burrville* (1968), *Abes Knoll* (1969), *Greenwich* (1969), *Parker Knoll* (1969), *Angle* (1970), *Phonolite Hill* (1971), *Junction* (1966), *Circleville* (1966), *Bull Rush Peak* (1966), *Fremont Pass* (1966), *Panguitch NW* (1966), *Little Creek Peak* (1971), *Cottonwood Mtn.* (1971), *Paragonah* (1971), *Parowan* (1971), *Summit* (1971), *Enoch* (1950), *Cedar City* (1950), *Cedar City NW* (1949), *The Three Peaks* (1950), *Avon SE* (1951), *Antelope Peak* (1950), *Silver Peak* (1950), *Newcastle* (1972), *Pinto* (1972), *Enterprise* (1972), *Central West* (1972), *Central East* (1972), *Veyo* (1972), *Gunlock* (1972), *Beaver Dam Mts. NE* (1954), *Beaver Dam Mts. SE* (1954).

Utah. 15 Minute Series (1:62,500).

> *Eastland* (1957), *Lisbon Valley* (1954), *Hatch Rock* (1954), *La Sal Junction* (1954), *Castle Valley* (1954), *Moab* (1959), *The Knoll* (1951), *Crescent Junction* (1958), *Green River* (1954), *Gunnison Butte* (1963), *Tidwell Bottoms* (1954), *Castle Dale* (1923), *Richfield* (1961), *Monroe* (1940), *Marysvale* (1945).

Arizona. 15 Minute Series (1:62,500).

> *Littlefield* (1954), *Mesquite* (1957).

Nevada. 15 Minute Series (1:62,500).

> *Mesquite* (1957), *Virgin Peak* (1958), *Overton* (1958), *Moapa* (1958), *Muddy Peak* (1953), *Dry Lake* (1952), *Henderson* (1952), *Las Vegas* (1952), *Blue Diamond* (1952), *Goodsprings* (1960), *Mountain Springs* (1957), *Shenandoah Peak* (1956), *Horse Thief Springs* (1956).

California. 7.5 Minute Series (1:31,250).

> *Baldy Mesa* (1956), *Cajon* (1956; photorevised, 1968 and 1973), *San Dimas* (1966; photorevised, 1972), *Baldwin Park* (1966; photorevised, 1972), *El Monte* (1966; photorevised, 1972), *Los Angeles* (1966; photorevised, 1972).

California. 15 Minute Series (1:62,500).

> *Horse Thief Springs* (1956), *Tecopa* (1950), *Silurian Hills* (1956), *Avawatz Pass* (1948), *Baker* (1956), *Red Pass Lake* (1948), *Cave Mountain* (1948), *Alvord Mountain* (1948), *Newberry* (1955), *Daggett* (1956), *Barstow* (1956), *Hawes* (1956), *Victorville* (1956), *San Bernardino* (1954), *Ontario* (1954).

Wheeler, George M.

1869-1873   *U.S. Geographical Surveys West of the 100th Meridian, Parts of E. California, S.E. Nevada, N.W. Arizona and S.W. Utah.* Atlas Sheet No. 66. Washington, D.C.: Expedition of 1869-1872, 1873.

———.

1882   *U.S. Geographical Surveys West of the 100th Meridian, Parts of Southern Colorado and Northern New Mexico.* Atlas Sheet No. 69. Washington, D.C.

———.

1883   *U.S. Geographical Surveys West of the 100th Meridian, Part of Southern California.* Atlas Sheet No. 73. Washington, D.C.

INDEX

Abajo or Blue Mountains, UT., 41, 43, 45, 46, *46*
Abiquiu, NM., 14, 16, *16,* 17
Agua de Tomaso. *See* Bitter Spring
Agua Escarbada. *See* Stump Spring
Alamo Ranch, CO., *37,* 38, 39
Alvord Mountain, CA., *109,* 110
Amargosa River, CA., 100–101, *101,* 102, *102*
Amargosa River Canyon Preserve, CA., 101
Anasazi Heritage Center, CO., *36, 37,* 40
Anasazi Indians, 26, 33, 37, 41, 43
Animas River, CO., 18, 26, 27, 28, *28,* 29, 81
Antelope Spring, UT., 72, *72*
Arboles, CO., 23, 24
Arches National Park, UT., 45, 51–52
Archilette Spring. *See* Resting Springs
Armijo, Antonio, 11
Arrowhead Trail, 86, 87, 115
Arroyo Seco, NM., 17
Avawatz Mountains, CA., 106

Barnes, F. A., 47
barrel cactus, 82–83
Barstow, CA., 110, 111, 113, 114
Beale, E. F., 56
Bear Valley, UT., 69
Beaver Dam, AZ., 75, 80
Beaver Dam Mountains, UT., 75, 78, 79
Beaver Dam Wash, AZ.–UT., 80, *80,* 93
Beckwith, E. G., 56
Big Holes, UT., *57,* 58, *58*
Bitter Spring, CA., 97, 106–110, *108*
Blue Diamond, NV., 92, *92,* 93
Book Cliffs, UT., 55, *55*
Brewerton, George D., 5, 65, 66, 73, 117
Bunkerville, NV., 81
Burford Lake, NM., 19, 21, *21*
Butt, H.U., 45

Cajon Pass, CA., 73, 86, 101, 111, 113, 114, 116,
    119, 119–121
California Crossing, NV., 85–86
California Desert Information Center, Barstow,
    CA., 113–114, *114*
California Road, 71, 86, *88*
California Valley, CA., 97, *97, 98*
California Wash, NV., 87
Camp Cady, CA., 108, *111,* 113

Camp Douglas, Salt Lake City, UT., 78
Camp Spring, UT., *78,* 78–79
Canyonlands National Park, UT., 45, 48, 52
Cañon Pintado, UT., *46,* 47
Capote Utes, 24
Carleton, James Henry, 108
Carlisle Cattle Company, 45
Carracas, CO., *21,* 22, *22* 23, 28
Carracas Canyon, NM., 21
Carrizo Mountains, CO., 30
Carson, Kit, 5, 65, 74, 99, 117
Carvalho, Solomon N., 88, 89–90, 105
Casa Colorado, UT., *46,*47, *47,* 48
Cassidy, Butch, 67, *67*
Castle Dale, UT., 60
Castle Valley, UT., 55, 59–60, *60,* 61
Cedar City, UT., 72
Cedar Mountain, UT., 59
Cedar Valley, UT., *70,* 72
Central, UT., 75
Chama River, NM., 13, 14
Chapin, F. H., 39
Cheesman, David W., 82, 121
Cherry Creek, CO., 30, 33
Chimayo, NM., *16*
Church of Jesus Christ of Latter-day Saints. *See*
    Mormons
Chuska Mountains, CO., 30
Circleville, UT., 67
Clear Creek, UT., 64–65
Colorado Plateau, 61, 66, 80
Colorado River, 11, 21, 34, 45, 47, 48, 49, 51, *51,* 67
Connor, Patrick Edward, 78
Continental Divide, 21, 23
Cortez, CO., 40–41, 42
Cottonwood Spring, NV., 92, 93
Coues, Elliott, 111
Courthouse Spring, UT., 52, *53*
Cross Canyon, CO., *41,* 42, *42,* 43
Crowder Canyon, CA., 120
Cucamonga, CA., 121–122, *121*

Dan O'Laurie Museum, 50–51
de Mofras, Duflot, 124
Death Valley National Monument, CA., 97,
    101–102
Denton, William, 106

Denver & Rio Grande Railroad, 23, 28, *58*
Dimmock, Charles, 16, 18, 41, 43, 46
Dolores Archaeological Salvage Project, 40
Dolores, CO., *33, 34,* 36
Dolores River, *25,* 34, 35, 36, 37, 40, 41
Dolores-Monticello Road, 36, 42, 43, 45, *45*
Domínguez, Francisco Atanasio, 10, 18, 25, 35, 40
Domínguez-Escalante Trail, 26, *71*
Dove Creek, CO., 43, *43*
Dulce, NM., 22
Durango, CO., 21, 22, 28, 36

East Canyon, UT. *See* Cañon Pintado
El Monte, CA., 123
El Vado, NM., 18, 19
Elk Mountain Mission 50, 58
Elsinore, UT., 64
Emigrant Pass, CA., 97, 98, *98, 99*
Enoch, UT., 71, 72
Escalante, Francisco Silvestre Vélez de, 10, 18, 25, 35, 40
Escalante Desert, UT., 72
Española, NM., 14

Ferron, Augustus D., 60
Fish Lake, UT., 63, *65,* 65–66
Fish Lake Route, 61, 63, 65–66
Flint, Thomas, 100, 107
Fork of Roads, CA., 110, *110,* 113, 115
Fort Irwin Military Reservation, CA., 109
Fort Lewis, CO., 22, 29, 45
Fort Lewis College, Durango, CO., 28
Fort Mohave, CA., 79, 110
Four Corners region, 40, 41
Frémont, John C., 5, 63, 67, 69, 71, 73, 75, 80, 85, 88, 89, 95, 98–99, 104, 106, 107, 114, 116
Fremont Indian State Park, UT., *64,* 65
Fremont Indians, 65
Fremont Pass, UT., 69, *69*

Galloping Goose, *34,* 37
Garcés, Francisco Tomas Hermenegildo, 10, 111, 114, 120
Garside, Sherwin (Scoop), 88
Gass, O. D., 91
genizaros, 15
Ghost Ranch, NM., 17, *19*
Glen Helen Regional Park, Devore, CA., 120
Glendale, NV., 83
Godey, Alex, 99
Grand Junction, CO., 14
Great Basin, 63, 66, 67, 73, 80
Great Sage Plain, 33, 45
Green River, UT., 11, 48, 53, 55, *55,* 56
Green River, UT., (town) 11, 25
Green River Desert, UT., 55

Gunlock, UT., 75
Gunnison, John W., 6, 52, 53, 63
Gunnison railroad survey, 52, 56, 57, 60, 113

Halfway Wash, NV., 81, 82
Hamblin, Jacob, 77, *78*
Hayden, Ferdinand V., 38
Hayden Survey, 6, *34,* 38, 47
Heap, Gwinn Harris, 56, 64, 69, 77, 90, 95, 98, 100, 103, 107, 115
Hernandez's Spring. *See* Resting Springs
Hesperus, CO., 30, *30*
Holmes, William H., 38
Holt Canyon, UT., 72, 73
Hunt, Elisha, 80
Hunt, Jefferson, 73, 89, 101, 102
Huntington, Oliver B., 58, 59, 63

Ignacio, CO., 24, 26, *27*
Ingalls, G. W., 78
Iron County, UT., 72
Iron Mission State Historical Monument, 72
Iron Springs, UT., 72
Ivie Creek, UT., 61, 63, 66

Jackson, William H., 38
Jicarilla Apache Indian Reservation, 21
John Brown Toll Road, CA., *119,* 120
John Wesley Powell River History Museum, *56,* 57
Johnson Valley Reservoir, UT., 65
Jones, A. H., 105
Joshua tree, 79, *79,* 116
Junction, UT., *65,* 66

Kane Springs, UT., 49
Kingston cutoff, NV.–CA., 104–105
Kingston Spring, CA., 104

La Plata Mountains, CO., 29
La Plata River, CO., 21, *25,* 29, 30, 31, 41
La Plata-Mancos Passage, CO, 34
La Sal Mountains, UT., 43, 45, *46,* 50, *50*
La Tinaja, UT., 47, *47,* 48
Lago Hediondo. *See* Burford Lake
Lake Mead, NV., 86, 87
Lane, A. G., 116
Lane's Crossing, CA., 116, *116*
Las Vegas, NV., 79, 85, 86, 89–92
Las Vegas Ranch (Mormon Fort), *90,* 91
Las Vegas Springs, NV., 89, 91, 92
Leroux, Antoine, 52
Lewis, CO., *38,* 41
Lions Club Park, Las Vegas, NV., 91
Little Grand Wash, UT., 52
Little Holes, UT., 59
Little Salt Lake, UT., *69,* 70, *74*

Looking Glass Rock, UT., 48, *49*
Los Angeles Old Plaza, 119, *123,* 124, *124,* 125
Los Pinos River, 24
Lost City Museum, NV., 87, *87*
Lytle, John, 88
Lytle Ranch, 80

Macomb military expedition, 6, 16, *18,* 27, 29, 35, 38, 42, 46
"Madonna of the Trail" monument, CA., *121,* 122, *122*
Mancos, CO., 33
Mancos River, CO., *25,* 33, 36
Markagunt Plateau, UT., 67, *67,* 69, 81
Marysvale, UT., 65
Mason, Charles, 39
Matheson, S. Alva, 72
McPhee Dam, 40
Meadow Canyon. *See* Holt Canyon
Mendenhall, W. C., 103
Mesa Verde, CO., 33, 38-40, 41
Mesa Verde National Park, CO., *35,* 37–40
Mesquite, NV., 81, 86
Miera y Pacheco, Bernardo, 18, 19, *25*
Moab, UT., 25, 45, 47, 50, 51, *51,* 58
Moapa Valley, NV., 85, *85,* 86
Mojave River, CA., 99, 111, 114–116, *115*
Mojave River Valley Museum, Barstow, CA., 114
Mojave Road, CA., 110
Monterey, CA., 10
Monticello Road. *See* Dolores-Monticello Road
Mormon Mesa, NV., 75, 81–82, *82, 83,* 86
Mormon Road, 71, 86, 113
Mormons, 45, 49, 50, 55, 59–60, 67, 69, 71, 72, 91
Moss, John, 30, 31, 38
Mountain Meadows, UT., 67, *73,* 73–74, 75, 78
Mountain Springs, NV., 93–94, *94, 95*
Mowry, Sylvester, 82
Muache Utes, 24
Muddy River, NV., 77, 83, *85,* 85–86, 87
Myhrer, Keith, 92

Narraguinnep Reservoir, CO., 41
National Old Trails Highway, 115, 122
Navajo State Recreation Area, 23, *24*
Nellis Air Force Base, NV., 87, 88
Nevada Centennial Trail Markers, 88–89, *89*
Nevada Historical Society, *91,* 91–92
Nevada State Museum, *91,* 91–92
Newberry, J. S., 29, 30, 33, 35, 36, 37, 38, 40, 42, 46, 47, 48
Newcastle, UT., 72
Newspaper Rock State Park, UT., 48, *48*
Nopah Range, CA., 97
Nordenskiold, Gustaf, 39

Ojo Verde, UT., 48
O'Keeffe, Georgia, 17

Old Spanish Trail Highway, 97, 98, *98*
Old Spanish Trail Ranch, 79
Oñate, Juan de, 10, 14-15
Oro Grande, CA., 114, 115
Otter Creek, UT., 66
Overton, NV., 87

Pagosa Springs, CO., 18
Pahrump Valley, NV.–CA., 95, *95,* 97
Paiute Indians, 11, 75, 77, 78, 85, 87
Palace of the Governors, *13,* 14
Palmer, William R., 71, 72
Paragonah, UT., 69, 70, 116
Parowan Valley, UT., 69, 70, 71, 73, 86
Parrott City, CO., 31
Pedernal, Cerro del, *18,* 19
Piedra Parada, CO., 18
Piedra River, 23, *25*
Pinto Creek, UT., 72
Piute Spring, UT., 45, *45,* 46
Pojaque, NM., 14
Potosi mine, 94, *94*
Powell, John Wesley, 57, *77,* 78
Pratt, Addison, 89, 100, 102
Pratt, Orville, 5, 27, 29, 30, 46, 51, 52, 55, 64, 69, 70, 73, 85, 95, 122
Pratt, Parley P., 99–100
Pratt, Parley P., exploring expedition 70
Price, George F., 78–79, 82
Price, UT., 58
Pueblo Revolt, 24
Puerta Grande, NM., 19, *19,* 21

Red Pass, CA., 106
Resting Springs, CA., 97, 98–100, *99, 100*
Richfield, UT., 64
Rio Animas. *See* Animas River
Rio Cebolla, NM., 18, 27
Rio Chama, NM. *See* Chama River
Rio Grand Southern Railroad, *34,* 36, 37
Rio Grande, 15, 21
Rio Nutrias, NM., 18
Rio Virgen. *See* Virgin River
Rivera, Juan Maria Antonio de, 25, 26, 34
Ruffner, E. H., 45

Salina Canyon, UT., 61, *63,* 63–64
Salt Spring, CA., 97, 103, 104, *106*
Salt Spring Gold Mines, CA., 103, *105*
San Bernardino, CA., 80
San Bernardino Mountains, CA., 116
San Gabriel, CA., *122,* 122–123, *123,* 124
San Gabriel, NM., 15, *15*
San Ildefonso Pueblo, NM., 14, *14*
San Juan Mountains, CO., 28, 31
San Juan National Forest, CO., 33
San Juan Pueblo, NM., 14, *15*

San Juan River, 21, 23, 33
San Rafael River, UT., 59
San Rafael Swell, UT., 53, 55, *57,* 58, *58,* 59, *59*
Sanford, William, 120
Santa Clara Pueblo, NM., 14
Santa Clara River, UT., 75, 77, 78
Santa Cruz, NM., 14, *14*
Santa Fe Railroad, 111, *113*
Santa Fe & Salt Lake Trail, 120
Sevier River, UT., 52, 61, 63, 64, *65,* 67, 69, 75
Shivwits Indian Reservation, 75
Shoshoni Indians, 25
Silurian Lake, CA., 104–106, *107*
Silver Lake, CA., 106
Smith, Jedediah, 10, 120, *122*
Smith, Thomas L. "Peg-Leg," 105
Southern Paiute Indians, 75
Southern Utah University, Cedar City, UT., 72
Southern Ute Indian Reservation, 24
Southern Utes, 24, 25–26
Spanish Canyon, CA., 110
Spanish Trail Association, 71
Spanish Trail, northern branch, 14
Spanish Valley, UT., 49
Spring Mountains, NV., 85, 93
Stewart, Helen, 91
Stinking Lake. *See* Burford Lake
Stump Spring, NV., 94–95
St. Jose (Saint Joseph) Spring, UT., 70–71
St. Louis Rock, UT., 49, *50*
Sublette, Andrew, 102
Sullivan-May Nature Center and Historic Site, CA., 120, *120*
Surouaro, CO., 42
Sycamore Grove, CA., *120,* 121

Taos, NM., 14
Taos Pueblo, NM., 14
Tecopa, CA., 100, *100, 102*
Tejon Pass, CA., 116
Tesuque Pueblo, NM., 14

Thompson, David G., 103, 106, 109
Thompson Park, CO., 33, *33*
Thomson, C. S. Cecil, 51
Tierra Blanca. *See* Cross Canyon
Tonopah and Tidewater Railroad, 100, *106*
Trail Spring, UT., *57,* 58
Treaty of Guadalupe-Hidalgo, 25

Ucolo, UT., *45,* 46
University of Nevada, Las Vegas, 92
Upland, CA., 122
Utah Hill, UT., *79,* 79–80, *80*
Ute Indians, 21, 24, 25, 34, 39, 50, 56, 75, 77
Ute Junction, CO., *23,* 29, 30

Valley of Fire State Park, NV., 86–87, *88*
Veyo, UT., *75*
Victorville, CA., 111, 114
Virgin Hill, NV., 81–82, *82, 83*
Virgin River, UT.–AZ.–NV., 75, 77, 78, 80–81, *81,* 82
von Egloffstein, F. W., 38, 43

Wade, Harry, family, 102
Wakara (Ute chief), 77
Wasatch Pass, UT., 60, 63
Wasatch Plateau, UT., 53, 59
Washington, Henry, 106
Weminuche Utes, 24
Wetherill, Richard, 39
Wheeler Survey, 6, 21, *21,* 93, 110, 123
Whipple, A. W., 113, 115
Wilson Gulch, CO., 26, 27, 28
Wiltse, S. C., 105
Wolkskill, William, 11

Yellow Jacket, CO., *39*
Yellow Jacket Ruin, CO., *39, 40,* 41, 42
Yermo, CA., 110
Yount, George C., 11

Zion National Park, UT., 81